Scotland in the Middle Ages
400–1450 AD

Richard Dargie
(Lecturer in History, Moray House Institute of Education)

Pulse Publications

Acknowledgements

The author and publisher wish to thank the following for permission to reproduce copyright material:

The Scottish National Portrait Gallery, Edinburgh: the cover

Historic Scotland: 1.1A; 1.7A; 3.1A; 3.1D; 3.4C; 4.5A; 5.4A; 6.6A,E,F; 7.3A; 7.5B; 9.7C; 10.10A and page 48.

Grampian Regional Council: 1.6A; 1.6B

Aberdeen District Council: 7.6A; 8.5A; 8.3A

Crown Copyright: Royal Commission on the Ancient and Historical Monuments of Scotland: 1.2A; 5.2A; 5.3A.

National Museums of Scotland: 1.4A; 1.4B; 2.3A; 2.5D; 2.7F; 5.6A.

The Trustees of the National Library of Scotland: 4.1B; 6.1C; 7.6B; 7.8B; 8.7A; 9.3C; 11.5A.

The Trustees of the British Museum: 1.5B.

Mack Picture Agency : 1.8A; 10.5A.

University Museum of National Antiquities, Oslo, Norway: 2.1B.

Melvin, Gould and Thompson, A New History of Scotland, John Murray (Publishers) Ltd: 4.7A; 5.3B; 8.4B.

Koninklijke Bibliotheek Albert I, Brussel, Belgie: 11.6F

The Directors of the Clydesdale Bank plc: 6.4A.

HMSO Scotland: 7.2A; 7.2B.

Resources for Environmental Studies Teaching (R.E.S.T.), Moray House Institute of Education: 8.2A; 8.7B

Special thanks to Donald Gunn, BBC Education, and Ken Reid, Moray House, for their valuable comments during the production of this book.

Publishers Note
Every effort has been been made to trace and acknowledge copyright holders, but if any have been inadvertently overlooked, the publisher will be pleased to make the appropriate arrangements at the first opportunity.

Published and Typeset by **Pulse Publications**
45 Raith Road, Fenwick, Ayrshire, KA3 6DB

Printed by **Ritchie** of Edinburgh

British Library Cataloguing-in-Publication Data
A Catalogue record for this book is available from the British Library

ISBN 0 948766 36 0

© **Richard Dargie 1995**

All rights reserved. No part of this publication may be reproduced, stored in a retrieval system, or transmitted in any form or by any means, electronic, mechanical, photocopying, recording or otherwise, without the written permission of the publisher.

Contents

Unit **One**	The Early Peoples of Scotland	5
Unit **Two**	The Vikings in Scotland	15
Unit **Three**	The Coming of the Cross	25
Unit **Four**	One Kingdom – Alba	32
Unit **Five**	The Normans in Scotland	41
Unit **Six**	In Time of War	49
Unit **Seven**	The Medieval Church	59
Unit **Eight**	Burgh Life	71
Unit **Nine**	Country Life	82
Unit **Ten**	The Wars with England	92
Unit **Eleven**	The Kynrik at Peace	108
Timeline		118
Index		119

To the teacher

Scotland in the Middle Ages is a new resource book which addresses the recommendation in Environmental Studies 5–14 that pupils should study Scottish history and the period 400 to 1450 AD. It contains carefully selected visual and written source material, and a text which emphasises explanation rather than simple narrative. The language level and pupil tasks in each unit have been graded throughout the book in the belief that this will provide opportunities for progression and enrichment in pupil attainment, and also opportunities for associated primary and secondary staffs to plan their joint use of this resource book on a collaborative basis. Although the book retains an overall chronological framework, it is structured around questions, issues, controversy and debate in Scottish History. As such, the use of this book will promote pupil skill development in Evaluating and Investigating and thereby serve as a comprehensive foundation for later progress at Standard Grade in the Social Subjects.

Scotland
in the Middle Ages

This map shows some of the main places and areas referred to in the book.

Unit 1

The Early Peoples of Scotland

1.1	What were the Middle Ages?	6
1.2	What was Scotland like in the early Middle Ages?	7
1.3	Who lived in Scotland in 400 AD?	8
1.4	Who were the Picts?	9
1.5	Where did the name Pict come from?	10
1.6	What was the Burghead Well?	11
1.7	What happened at Nechtansmere?	12
1.8	Why did the Picts vanish?	13
1.9	Why did the Picts and Scots unite into one nation?	14

1.1 What were the Middle Ages?

THIS book is about Scotland at a time in the past called the Middle Ages. Look at the *Contents* on page 3 and see what the units in the book are about. The title of the book tells you when the Middle Ages were. The names of the units give you an idea of what happened in the Middle Ages, what kind of people lived then, and what their lives were like. You will be reading and learning about people who lived in Scotland between the years 400 and 1450 AD.

Historians give names to different periods or ages in the past. The years before 400 AD are usually called ancient times or the classical period. This is the time of peoples like the ancient Egyptians and the Romans. Most historians agree that this period came to an end around the year 400.

Many new things began in Europe after the year 1450. Explorers made long voyages to learn more about the world. There were important discoveries in sciences like chemistry and astronomy. This was the beginning of the modern period in which we still live today.

The years between 400 and 1450 in Europe are called the Middle Ages.

Source A: Edinburgh Castle in the Middle Ages

Things to Do

1. Put a heading *The Three Ages of European History* into your jotter. Copy the diagram below. Fill in the name of each period in the correct box.

2000 BC	400 AD	1450 AD	2000 AD

2. In your own words, explain why the years between 400 and 1450 AD are called the Middle Ages.

3. Look at Source A which shows one of the most important places in Scotland in the Middle Ages. What does this Source tell you about life at that time?

1.2 What was Scotland like in the early Middle Ages?

Source A: Early hill fort, Islay

SCOTLAND was a very different country in the early Middle Ages. Much of the lower land was covered in great bogs. There were vast marshes near rivers and lochs where the land was poorly drained. The higher ground was covered by moor or thick tangled forest. The mountain areas in the north and west were wild and uninhabited. This was where the wild creatures of Scotland—the eagle, red deer, wild boar and the packs of grey wolves—roamed.

There were few signs of the human population. No proper roads through this rough country existed, just tracks or paths. You had to know where it was safe to ford, or walk across, Scotland's many streams and rivers as there were no bridges.

Very few people lived in Scotland in 400 AD. There was very little farmland and no proper towns. Instead, small settlements grew up near safe places like the fortress rocks at Dunadd in Argyll or Traprain Law in East Lothian. The population was thinly spread out. Most people lived on the coasts near the sea, or close to inland rivers.

Things to Do

1. Make a list of the ways in which Scotland in 400 AD was different from Scotland today.

2. Look at Source A.
   (a) Why did the early people of Scotland live close to places like this?
   (b) What would be the advantages and disadvantages of living in a hill fort?
   (c) Why do you think many people lived on the coast or near rivers?

3. Use an atlas or map to find the following fortress rocks or hill forts. Fill them in on a blank map of Scotland.

   Dunadd; Traprain Law; Edinburgh Rock; Tap o' Noth; Dumbarton Rock.

Scotland in the Middle Ages 400 – 1450 AD

1.3 Who lived in Scotland in 400 AD?

IN 400 AD most people in Scotland lived in farm villages in groups of about thirty or forty. They struggled to raise enough crops and animals to live on. Food could also be found by hunting in the great marshes and forests which covered much of the land. The rivers and the sea shore were other places where food could be found and caught.

The first peoples in Scotland belonged to tribes ruled by a chief. Many tribes had a safe place like a hill fort to run to in times of danger. Most villages were close to hill forts. Some tribes were Christian. They had been converted by the first missionaries such as St Ninian and St Kentigern. However, these peoples were often at war with each other, so chiefs and warriors were important members of the tribe.

The Picts were tribal people who lived in Scotland in 400 AD. The Pictish kings were the most powerful in Scotland. They ruled most of the country north of the Forth and Clyde valleys. By 600 AD the Britons had built a strong kingdom around the Clyde river and in the south west. However, by 650 the powerful Angles of Northumbria had pushed their way into south eastern Scotland and captured the important rock fortress of Din Eidyn (Edinburgh).

As early as the year 500, an Irish tribe had crossed over the sea to settle in Argyll. They called their new kingdom in Scotland 'Dalriata'. The tribe were called 'scots', meaning raiders, by their enemies. In the year 843 the leader of these Scots, Kenneth MacAlpin, also became king of the Picts. Much of the country was now united into one kingdom. In the Gaelic language of the Scots this kingdom was called Alba, but in the language of Latin used across Europe it was known as Scotia.

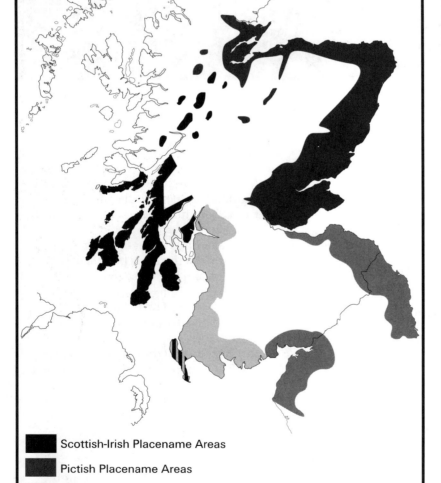

- Scottish-Irish Placename Areas
- Pictish Placename Areas
- Anglian-Northumbrian Placename
- British Placename Areas

Source A: Placenames of the Picts, Scots, Britons and Angles

Things to Do

1. In your jotter put a heading *The Four Early Peoples of Scotland*. Copy or draw a blank map of Scotland. Use the information in the text and in Source A to mark in where the Picts, Britons, Angles and Scots had their kingdoms. You may need an atlas to help you.

2. Use your class or school library to find out more about the Britons and the Angles. Find out where they came from and what sort of things they have left behind.

Scotland in the Middle Ages 400 – 1450 AD

1.4 Who were the Picts?

THE PICTS were people who lived in much of northern and eastern Scotland between 200 and 850 AD. They were probably descended from the early Celts who were one of the first people to settle Britain.

The Picts knew how to work metals and were skilled stone carvers. They had a kind of writing called ogam script. By the year 600 the Picts had kings who were Christian. However, there are many things we do not know about the Picts. We think they were divided up into separate tribes. One tribe had its capital in the great fortress of Burghead in Morayshire. We know the names of the seven largest Pictish kingdoms.

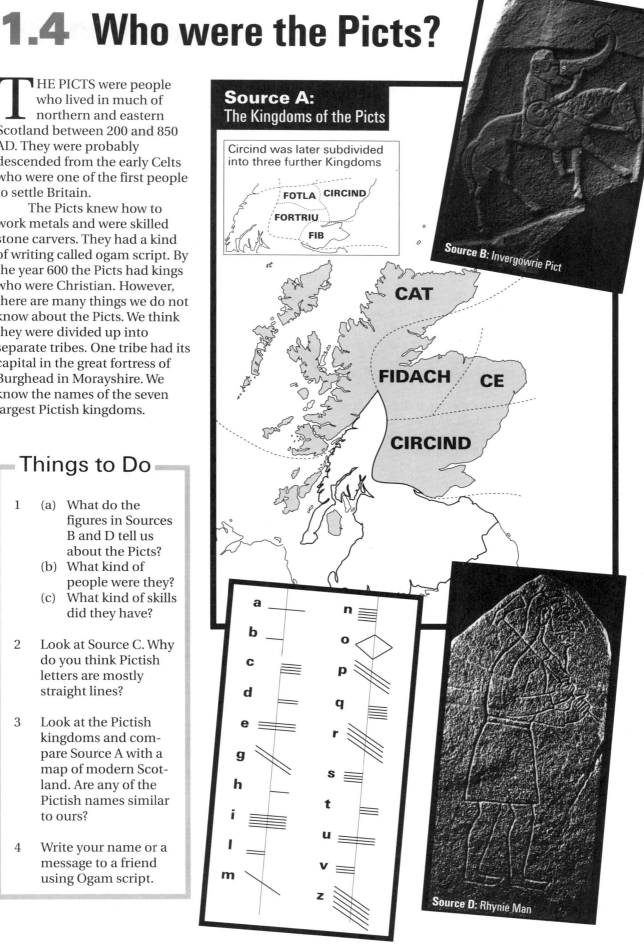

Source A: The Kingdoms of the Picts

Circind was later subdivided into three further Kingdoms (FOTLA, CIRCIND, FORTRIU, FIB)

CAT, FIDACH, CE, CIRCIND

Source B: Invergowrie Pict

Source C: The Ogam alphabet

Source D: Rhynie Man

Things to Do

1. (a) What do the figures in Sources B and D tell us about the Picts?
   (b) What kind of people were they?
   (c) What kind of skills did they have?

2. Look at Source C. Why do you think Pictish letters are mostly straight lines?

3. Look at the Pictish kingdoms and compare Source A with a map of modern Scotland. Are any of the Pictish names similar to ours?

4. Write your name or a message to a friend using Ogam script.

Scotland in the Middle Ages 400 – 1450 AD

1.5 Where did the name Pict come from?

WE DO NOT know what the Picts called themselves. Their alphabet survives, but not their language. We can read the messages they carved on stone, but we do not know what they mean. All that we have are the names which they were called by their enemies.

The word *Picti* first appeared in a Latin poem written in 297 AD. Some early historians thought this meant 'the painted ones'. There is a long-standing legend that the tribes north of Hadrian's Wall painted or tattooed their bodies, but the early written records do not mention this custom.

It is more likely that the name comes from an ancient celtic word *pett*. In the old languages of Welsh and Cornish, *pett* or *pit* means a piece or share of land. It appears in many place names in areas such as Perthshire, Fife, and Aberdeenshire settled by Pictish tribes.

English chroniclers writing in the 7th and 8th centuries usually called their northern enemies the *Pehtas*. In the Norse sagas, the tribes of northern Scotland are called the *Pettar*. The Viking seaway between Scotland and the Orkneys was called *Pettlandsfjord*.

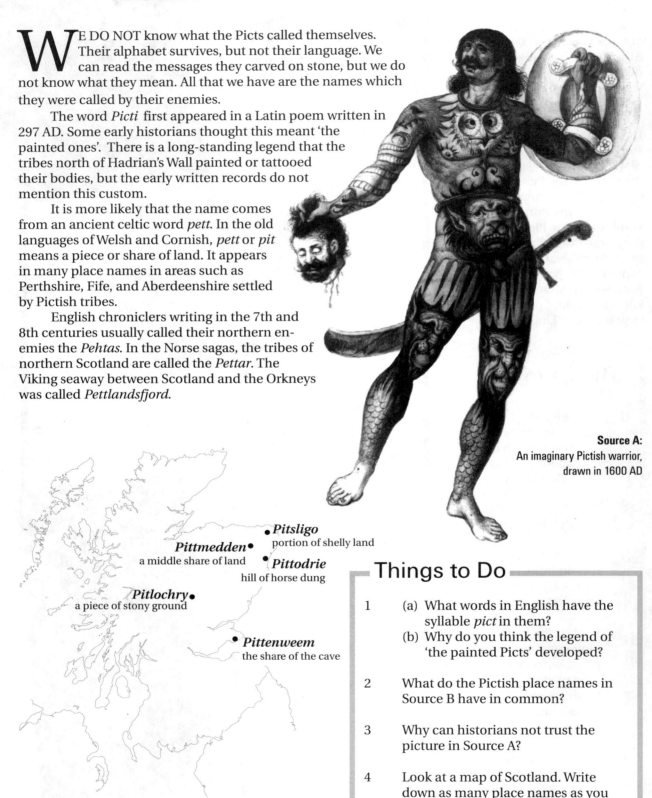

Source A: An imaginary Pictish warrior, drawn in 1600 AD

Pitsligo – portion of shelly land
Pittmedden – a middle share of land
Pittodrie – hill of horse dung
Pitlochry – a piece of stony ground
Pittenweem – the share of the cave

Source B: Pictish place names and their likely meanings

Things to Do

1. (a) What words in English have the syllable *pict* in them?
   (b) Why do you think the legend of 'the painted Picts' developed?

2. What do the Pictish place names in Source B have in common?

3. Why can historians not trust the picture in Source A?

4. Look at a map of Scotland. Write down as many place names as you can find with *pit* or *pet* in them.

Scotland in the Middle Ages 400 – 1450 AD

1.6 What was the Burghead Well?

ON THE Moray coast is the modern village of Burghead. It lies on a spur of land sticking out into the sea. In Pictish times it was an important settlement. It was protected by a series of ditches and earth walls or ramparts. There was an inner fort made of stone walls, but in the 1700s these walls were taken down. The stone was used to build the local harbour.

Old records mentioned that the walls had thirty carvings on them, each one of a powerful bull. Possibly bulls were the symbol of a local Pictish leader or a god, but the actual meaning of the carvings is not known. It was thought that the Burghead stones were lost forever. However, in recent years six of these mysterious carvings have been rediscovered, although the others are still lost.

There is a greater mystery at Burghead however. In the middle of the old fort is a flight of twenty steps cut in the rock. They lead down underground into a black hole. In the dark is a massive square chamber. There is a platform, a basin and a pedestal, all cut from the solid rock. The chamber is a water well, but it is too big just to be a water supply. It has been built with great care and is the largest structure to survive from Pictish times. The Celts, ancestors of the Picts, believed in water gods. The Picts of Burghead may have believed in these old gods long after their cousins in the south of Scotland had become Christian.

THE Pictish stone cross at Glamis, Angus contains a most curious carving. Only the legs of an upturned human figure can be seen. The rest is in a large cauldron or well, as if the centre of a ritual baptism, or a grisly execution.

Source C: From a 19th century tourist guide to Scotland

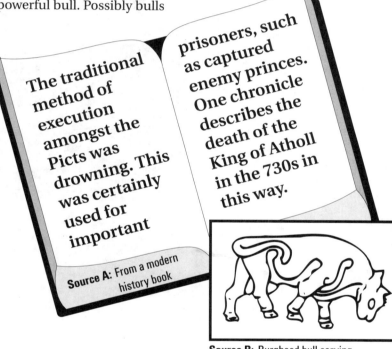

The traditional method of execution amongst the Picts was drowning. This was certainly used for important prisoners, such as captured enemy princes. One chronicle describes the death of the King of Atholl in the 730s in this way.

Source A: From a modern history book

Source B: Burghead bull carving

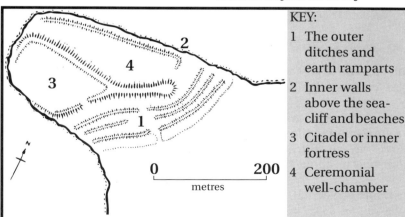

KEY:
1. The outer ditches and earth ramparts
2. Inner walls above the sea-cliff and beaches
3. Citadel or inner fortress
4. Ceremonial well-chamber

Source D: The Pictish fortress at Burghead

Things to Do

1. Why do you think a fortress was built at Burghead?

2. What evidence suggests that the Picts of Burghead were pagan?

3. Read Sources A and C. What do you think the Burghead Well was used for? Can we tell for sure, or can we only guess?

Scotland in the Middle Ages 400 – 1450 AD

1.7 What happened at Nechtansmere?

NECHTANSMERE was a great battle which took place in 685 AD near Forfar. Some historians believe it was the most important battle in Scotland's history. It was fought between the Picts and an invading army. The invaders were the powerful Angles from Northumbria.

The Angles were a Germanic people who had crossed the North Sea and settled in northern England. The Angles or Northumbrians had able leaders such as Bishop Wilfrid of York. He wanted to conquer the Picts. After 600 AD the Angles began to push northwards. By 640 they had destroyed the Celtic kingdom of Gododdin in what is today the Lothians. In 685 a huge Northumbrian army under King Ecgfrith marched north of Perth into Angus.

They were met near Forfar by a Pictish army led by a British chief, Bridei. The invaders were crushed and their king was killed. The invasion of northern Britain by the Angles was halted. They still occupied much of eastern Scotland south of the river Forth, but most of the country remained in Pictish, British or Scottish hands. Once they were united, these tribes would fight back.

Source A: The Aberlemno Stone

Things to Do

1. We think the Aberlemno Stone in Source A was carved by Picts after their victory at Nechtansmere in 685. Suggest a reason why the Picts might have done this.

2. Imagine you are an archaeologist who is studying the Picts. Write a short report on the Battle of Nechtansmere using the information in the text and the evidence on the Aberlemno Stone. In your report you should say why the battle was fought, why you think this stone was carved and also what the stone tells us about Pictish warriors and how they fought.

3. (a) Can you explain why the Battle of Nechtansmere was so important for the future of Scotland?
   (b) What might have happened if the Picts had been defeated?

1.8 Why did the Picts vanish?

IN THE year 750 AD the Picts ruled the largest kingdom in Scotland. A hundred years later their kingdom had vanished. The reason for this is not known but historians have made several guesses.

In the 790s the fierce Vikings or Norsemen began to raid the northern coasts of Scotland. They took over large parts of the Pictish kingdom such as Orkney, Shetland, Caithness and Sutherland. The old Pictish stronghold in Moray, the fortress of Burghead, was smashed by Norse invaders in the 9th century.

At the same time, the Vikings were attacking the western kingdom of the Scots, Dalriata. To survive, the Scots pushed eastwards into Perthshire and Angus as far as Brechin. Historians think that the Picts also lost a series of battles, and kings, in the 830s and early 840s. Whatever happened, they had a new Scottish king, Kenneth MacAlpin, by 843 AD. Within a generation or two, the language and traditions of the Picts had died out.

Source A: Tower at Brechin, 850 AD

The new Scottish rulers may have deliberately stamped out Pictish customs. Churches in Pictland were given new saints. Iona was abandoned for Dunkeld, the new religious heart of the kingdom. No Pictish books or written records survive. It is as if they were systematically destroyed by the new master race.

Source B: Written by a modern historian

In fact the Pictish lands may have been shrinking even before the Vikings arrived in Scotland. Maybe plague or famine had forced them to abandon some settlements in outlying areas.

Source C: Written by a modern historian

Things to Do

1. Read Sources B and C.
   (a) Why do you think the Pictish kingdom vanished? Give at least two reasons for your answer.
   (b) Why do you think the new Scottish kings wanted to stamp out the Pictish language?
   (c) What would they gain from doing this?

2. What do you think the tower at Brechin, shown in Source A, was used for? Give a reason for your answer.

1.9 Why did the Picts and Scots unite into one nation?

VERY few written records survive from the early Middle Ages. Often historians have to try and work out what happened with very little evidence to help them. They have to make clever guesses or theories. Sometimes new evidence is discovered which proves that older ideas are wrong. Historians also ask questions which help them to come up with new ways of explaining the past. You can see how this happens if you read the theories below. They show the changing way that historians have tried to answer the question at the top of this page.

The Historian

Volume 1   Issue No. 1

Uniting into one nation

The theory popular with historians around 1900 AD

ACCORDING to the old chronicles, Picts, Scots and British tribes fought each other for several centuries to have control of the mainland. The Picts were by far the strongest power in the land. Then their kingdom suddenly collapsed. In 839 AD the Picts had to fight three enemies at once: the Scots in the west, the Angles in the south and the Vikings everywhere around the coasts. Many of their leaders and best warriors were killed by the Vikings in a terrible defeat. While the Picts were still weak, the leader of the Scots, Kenneth MacAlpin, marched into Pictland with a huge army. He conquered the Picts, forcing them to surrender and accept him as their king in 843 AD. From then on the Picts were part of the Scottish nation.

The theory popular with present day historians

ALTHOUGH there were important differences between them, Picts and Scots lived similar lives and faced similar problems. Both had to fight off the Vikings and the Angles of Northumbria. They often joined together to fight their common enemies. It is clear from the archaeological evidence that, in times of peace, Picts and Scots traded with each other. The chronicles tell us that their ruling families often intermarried and Kenneth MacAlpin may have had blood from both tribes in his veins. He may have been asked by the Picts to lead them and save them from the Viking threat. He was not the first king to rule both Picts and Scots, but he was a very successful leader whose family or dynasty ruled Scotland well for several centuries to come.

Things to Do

1. What is different about these two theories?

2. Are there any points which are the same in both versions?

3. What evidence are the theories based on?

4. Why might old written records like chronicles be misleading?

5. Which of the two theories seems more convincing to you? Say why.

Unit 2
The Vikings in Scotland

2.1	Who were the Vikings?	16
2.2	Why did the Vikings come to Scotland?	17
2.3	Why did the Vikings attack Iona?	19
2.4	How do we know where the Vikings settled in Scotland?	20
2.5	Who were the great Jarls?	21
2.6	What was Viking life in Scotland like?	22
2.7	Raiders or traders?	23
2.8	What happened to the Vikings of Scotland?	24

2.1 Who were the Vikings?

THE VIKINGS or Norsemen came from Scandinavia. Most of the Vikings who sailed to Scotland originally came from Norway. This was a bleak, mountainous country with very little good soil for farming. The Norsemen had a hard time feeding their people in this harsh land. The sea cut deep inlets into their coastline and so the Norsemen had to be good fishermen and sailors to survive.

By the 790s the people of Norway did not have enough food for their growing population. They could not grow enough crops, so they decided to look for other lands where they could trade or plunder.

The first Viking raids to Scotland were in 795 AD. The Vikings terrified the Picts and the Scots. After 800 AD however, Viking farmers and their families began to settle in the islands of Orkney and Shetland, and in Caithness in the far north of Pictland. By the year 850, the Hebrides had become Viking lands. They called them the Sudreys or southern islands.

The early Vikings were pagan warriors, who worshipped the old Germanic gods Odin, Thor, Tew and Freya. They respected courage, strength and cunning. Nevertheless, by 950 AD many of the Viking settlers in Scotland had become Christian.

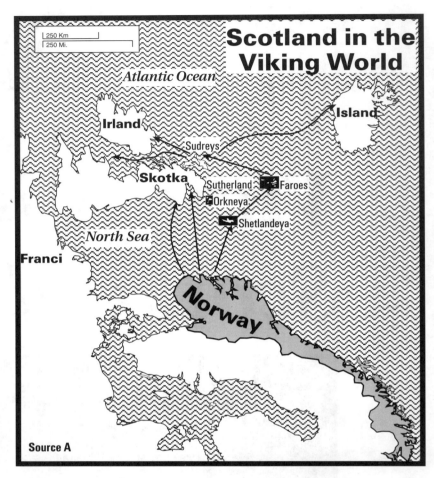

Source A

Things to Do

1. Why did the Norsemen find it hard to feed their people? What did this force them to do?

2. Look at Source A. Why did the Vikings choose Scotland as a place to trade and plunder?
   Now look at Source B. Why do you think the Picts and Scots were terrified of the Vikings?

3. Why do you think the Vikings decided to settle in the Orkney and Shetland islands?

4. How did the Vikings change their way of life after they had settled in Shetland?

5. Find out more about the old Viking gods. How are they remembered today?

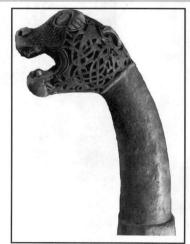

Source B: A Viking carving from a ship burial

Scotland in the Middle Ages 400 – 1450 AD

2.2 Why did the Vikings come to Scotland?

THERE are very few written sources which survive from the time of the first Viking raids. No-one can tell for sure why the Vikings decided to attack and settle in Scotland. Historians have come up with several theories or ideas to try and answer this question.

"According to some of the Viking sagas, the first Vikings were outlaws who fled from Norway at a time when the Norse kings were strong and were laying down the law. These outlaws came to Scotland so that they could carry on making a living by theft, slaving, looting and murder. There were many law-abiding Norse farmers and fishers who did not go on the Viking raids."

Historian A

"The Norse Vikings depended for much of their food on great shoals of cod and herring which lived in the North Sea. Unfortunately these shoals migrated and moved away from Norway towards Scotland. The first Vikings followed the fish westwards, then realised they could easily attack unprotected churches and villages in Scotland."

Historian B

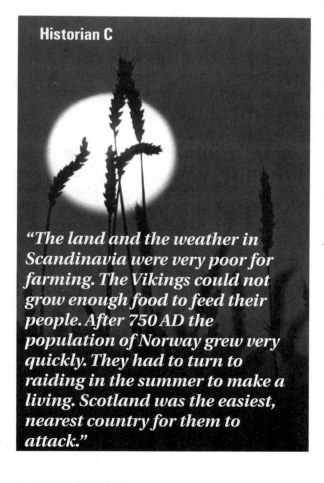

Historian C

"The land and the weather in Scandinavia were very poor for farming. The Vikings could not grow enough food to feed their people. After 750 AD the population of Norway grew very quickly. They had to turn to raiding in the summer to make a living. Scotland was the easiest, nearest country for them to attack."

"Later Vikings were mostly merchants and traders. They exchanged the forest products of northern Europe such as pelts and amber for oil and grain from the Mediterranean. Dublin in Ireland was one of their main trading centres. They settled in the islands around Scotland as a way of making sure they controlled the important trade routes across the seas. They needed safe harbours for their ships along the rocky coasts of Scotland on the long haul from Dublin to Orkney."

Historian D

Scotland in the Middle Ages 400 – 1450 AD

"The Norsemen attacked Scotland in the 790s because that was when they perfected their super-weapon, the longship. Earlier Norse ships could not have got across the stormy North Sea. However, by the 790s the Vikings had longships tough and fast enough to make summer raiding possible."

Historian E

"The Norsemen had visited northern Pictland before 795 AD. They knew the Pictish kingdoms had been badly weakened, maybe by civil war or by disease. The Vikings moved into empty lands which the Picts had deserted. Archaeologists think that the Vikings were often accepted peacefully as the new rulers in Northern Scotland. The local Pictish people had no strength left to fight these strong invaders. There is little evidence of a war between the Picts and the Norse."

Historian F

"The first Viking raiders were pagans who worshipped violent gods. They despised the weak monks and priests who served the peaceful god they called 'the White Christ'. They knew the monasteries, abbeys and churches of Christian Scotland contained great treasure. They also knew it would be easy to attack these poorly defended places."

Historian G

Things to Do

1. List the five reasons given to explain why the Vikings came to Scotland.

2. Which theory or reason do you think is most likely to be correct? Give reasons for your answer.

3. Which of the theories above is the closest to the explanation given in Unit 2.1 on page 16?

Scotland in the Middle Ages 400 – 1450 AD

2.3 Why did the Vikings attack Iona?

IN 795 AD Viking raiders attacked the Christian monastery on Iona. They returned in 802 and 806, killing 68 monks during their third raid on the island. In the year 825 they demanded that the monks hand over the sacred relics of St Columba which were kept in the monastery. When the monk Blathmac refused to say where this holy treasure had been hidden, the Vikings put him to the terrible death of blood-eagling. His chest was cut open, his ribs were torn apart and his lungs ripped out.

The Vikings attacked many monasteries throughout Europe, but why did Iona suffer so much?

Iona was the holiest Christian place in northern Britain. The bones of St Columba, who was honoured by Picts and Scots alike, were kept in a special box or reliquary at Iona. Pilgrims and great kings visited Iona and gave gifts to the monastery. Over the years, Iona became a centre of great wealth.

Today, Iona seems an out-of-the-way place, far from the main cities of our time. However, in the early Middle Ages, Iona was at the centre of all that was going on. Dozens of ships passed the island each year in the summer months. Their captains stopped to ask for a blessing on their voyage, and also left gifts as an offering to the Church.

The Vikings were slave traders and hostage takers. Monks were learned, educated men with valuable skills. Often they were members of wealthy and powerful families who could pay a ransom to free an important captive.

The Norsemen were superstitious people who believed in magic. They often attacked shrines which held relics of great holy power. Iona had many important religious objects which the Vikings wanted to have and control.

Source A: The reliquary of St Columba

Things to Do

1. In your own words give three reasons why the Vikings attacked Iona.

2. Study Source A.
   (a) What does it contain?
   (b) Why do you think this object was so important to Scottish people in the early Middle Ages?
   (c) Why did the Vikings try to capture this object?

3. Imagine you live in Scotland in the year 825 AD. You have just heard the news of the latest Viking raid on Iona. Write to a friend describing the events that took place there and your feelings about what has happened. Explain to your friend why you think the Vikings chose to raid Iona.

2.4 How do we know where the Vikings settled in Scotland?

HISTORIANS and archaeologists can use different kinds of evidence to prove where the Vikings lived in Scotland.

Firstly, many Viking burials have been discovered in Scotland. We can tell a lot from the grave goods that were buried alongside the dead Norseman or woman.

Clusters of Viking graves in one area tell us that this was a place where many Norsemen settled. Viking words in place names are another important clue. There are hundreds of places in Scotland which have Norse names. Many places in Scotland are also mentioned in the old Norse tales or sagas.

Things to Do

1. Look at Source A. What does this map tell you about where Vikings settled in Scotland?

2. Using an atlas, find the places mentioned in Source C. How are they similar? Why do you think Vikings settled in these places?

3. Using a map of Scotland, look for the names of places which have Viking words in them.

4. Look at the evidence from the sagas, place names and grave sites. Make a list of all the parts of Scotland which were settled by the Vikings. What do these places have in common?

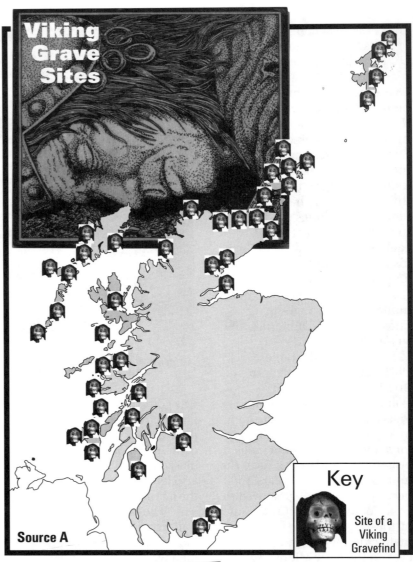

Source A

Key — Site of a Viking Gravefind

Norse Word	Place Name
kirkja	church
boll or pool	farm
vik or wik	bay or harbour
bister	farm
dale	valley
howe	mound

Source B: Norse words that appear in Scottish place names

Source C: From the saga of Magnus Bareleg written in 1100 AD

> The hungry battle-birds were filled,
> in Skye with blood of foemen killed,
> And wolves on Tiree's lonely shore,
> dyed red their hairy jaws in gore.
> The men of Mull were tired of flight,
> the Scottish foemen would not fight,
> And many an island girl's wail,
> was heard as through the Isles we sail.

Scotland in the Middle Ages 400 – 1450 AD

2.5 Who were the great Jarls?

THE JARLS, or Earls, were the Norse rulers of the northern isles. Some were men of great power who fed and kept large bands of warriors in their long halls or palaces. For a time, the small tidal island of Brough of Birsay in Orkney was the capital of the Earldom. No food was grown or prepared by the Vikings on this strong-point. It was brought to them by the local people who lived outside the palace across the bay.

The Jarls had colourful nicknames, such as Thorfinn Skull-splitter, which described their power. Earl Turf Einar got his name when he ordered his people to burn dried turfs of peat as a fuel on the treeless Orkneys.

Many of the Earls had poets, called skalds in Norse. These skalds were employed to tell tales or sagas, and record the deeds of their master. Many of these skaldic poems survive.

> Earl Thorfinn was famous because he entertained his men throughout the winter so that no one had to go to an inn. He provided all the food and drink needed at his own expense.

Source A: From the Orkney Saga

> There was no warrior as brave or as cunning as our mighty earl. There was no leader so loved by his people. There was no father so generous to his sons.

Source B: From a skaldic poem

> Earl Sigurd led his men straight into the heart of the Irish foe, holding aloft the magic banner of the black raven, fearing neither injury nor death, for no sword or axe could harm him.

Source C: From a skaldic poem

Things to Do

1. (a) Who were the Jarls?
   (b) What can we learn about the Jarls from the sagas and skaldic poems?
   (c) Would records like these really tell us the truth?
   (d) Why might the skaldic writers exaggerate the events and people they describe? Give a reason for your answer.

2. Write down at least two things about the Vikings that we can tell from the chessman discovered on the Isle of Lewis. (see source D)

3. Find the following book in your school or public library: *Viking Scotland* by Anna Ritchie published by Historic Scotland in 1993. Use this book to find out more about the Lewis chessmen. Write a short report saying where they were found, what they were made of and where they came from.

Source D: Viking chessman discovered on the Isle of Lewis

Scotland in the Middle Ages 400 – 1450 AD

2.6 What was Viking life in Scotland like?

The Historian

Volume 1

SPECIAL ON BIRSAY

Archaeologists have found out a lot about the way the Norsemen lived in Scotland. A number of important Viking sites have been excavated. The main ones are at Gurness and Brough of Birsay in Orkney, and at Jarlshof in Shetland.

Source A

BIRSAY is a tidal island in the Orkneys, cut off by the sea for much of the time. It can only be reached by a causeway at low tide. It was an easy site to defend but had beaches where the longships could be drawn up and repaired. There was an important Norse settlement here from around 800 to 1150 AD. We think that the Vikings moved to the island when an earlier Pictish community died out.

The 'Viking Palace' was right on the edge of the island, above a short stubby cliff.

Archaeologists have found a lot of evidence of Norse life on the island. Many of the objects found here suggest wealth and some degree of luxury. Pieces of weapon, pieces of cooking tools, pieces of clothing, pieces of jewellery and later, pieces of glass; all were made with care and were often decorated. They also found the ruins of several buildings (see Source B below).

There is very little fertile land on Birsay and no evidence that the Norse settlers farmed there. Some historians believe that the Brough of Birsay Vikings were warriors who forced the farmers on the nearby mainland to give them food and stores. They think that the long halls on the island were part of a palace where the Jarls held court and feasted with their men. Other writers think that the ruins were built by later Christian Jarls who encouraged monks from southern Scotland to build a small monastery there.

Gurness Finds	Jarlshof Finds	Brough of Birsay finds
iron shield bosses	a long-halled dwelling	several long-halled houses
a weighing balance	several farm buildings	several multi-roomed houses
a glass linen-smoother	five iron spearheads	a smithy
women's jewellery	several whetstones	two bath houses or saunas
two oval bronze brooches	soapstone bowls	the ruins of a church
pieces of a woollen dress	carved bone dresspins	a graveyard
an iron necklet	several bone sewing pins	a kiln for drying corn
an iron knife	three bronze ornaments	bone combs
an iron sickle	fishing hooks	bone amulets

Source B

Things to Do

1. Read Sources A and B. Use a dictionary to make sure you know what all the items in the list are. Work out what they were used for.

2. Use the information on this page to write a short report on 'Viking Life in Scotland'. Say what you can about what the Vikings wore, how they fed themselves, and what they worked at. Use the evidence in Sources A and B to *prove the points* that you make in your report.

3. Do you think Viking life in Scotland was exciting or hard work? Explain your answer.

4. Has the evidence in Sources A and B changed the way you think about the Vikings? Give a reason for your answer.

2.7 Raiders or traders?

> *Never before has such a terror appeared in Britain as we have now suffered from this pagan race... from the fury of the Norsemen, deliver us O Lord.*

Source A: From the Lindisfarne Chronicle written by a Christian monk

UNTIL recently, most historians usually described the Vikings as just raiders and pirates. This was because historians relied on a few old written records or chronicles. These chronicles were written at the time of the Viking raids by Christian monks who hated and feared the pagan Norsemen. Some modern historians have a different view of Viking life. They have found evidence that shows the peaceful things which the Norsemen did in Scotland. We now realise that the Vikings were settled in Scotland for over five hundred years. The Vikings changed a great deal in that time.

By the 1300s the men of Orkney had become peaceful farmers and fishermen. In turn they suffered from pirate attacks, this time from Irish and Hebridean raiders. Orkney was savaged in 1461 and many local people were taken into slavery. For the descendants of the Vikings, the wheel had come full circle.

Source B: From a history book

The Vikings were barbaric pirates who despised learning. We will never know what treasures of knowledge were lost when the great library at Iona was burnt to the ground.

Source C: From a history book

Med logum skal land byggia

Through the law the land shall flourish

Source D: The old Norse motto of Shetland

"This is how Svein used to live on Orkney. He spent winter at home on Gairsay, where he fed and kept eighty men at his own expense. His drinking hall was huge, there was nothing like it elsewhere in Orkney. In the spring he was busy, making sure that the seed was sown carefully. When that was done, he would go off plundering in the Hebrides and Ireland on what he called his 'spring-trip'. He was home by mid-summer, where he stayed until the corn was safely harvested. After that he went off raiding again on his 'autumn-trip', until the first month of winter."

Source F: From the Saga of the Orkneys

Source E: Arabic coins found at Skaill

Things to Do

1. Which of the sources presents the Vikings as peaceful people?

2. What do these sources tell you about how Viking activity in Scotland changed between the years 795 and 1300?

3. The coins shown in Source E were minted in Arabia but discovered in a Viking grave in Orkney. What does this tell you about the Vikings as traders?

4. Read and discuss the Sources A, B, C, D and F with a friend. Put them in what you think is the right order by date.

Scotland in the Middle Ages 400 – 1450 AD

2.8 What happened to the Vikings of Scotland?

BY THE year 1000 AD most of the Norse folk in Scotland had become Christians. They mixed and intermarried with the local population. This island race lived a long way from the growing towns on the mainland. They took little notice of the king of Scotland and his laws. However, they also lived far from their Norse roots and rulers. Even the great Norwegian king, Magnus Bareleg, had to lead an expedition to the Scottish isles to enforce his rule.

By the 1200s the Scottish kings in the south had grown powerful enough to try to win back land from the Norsemen. King William the Lion (1165–1214) began the reconquest of Caithness, Ross and Sutherland. In 1263 King Haakon IV of Norway attacked the west coast of Scotland with a huge fleet of 150 ships, but at Largs he lost many of them in a storm and his army was shipwrecked. Surrounded by the Scots, the stranded Norsemen ran out of food, starved and fell sick. A few were rescued, but Haakon died soon afterwards at Kirkwall in the Orkneys. His son sold the Hebrides to the Scots in 1266 for 4000 merks and a yearly 'quit-rent' of 100 merks.

The rights to Orkney and Shetland were also pawned to Scotland in 1468–69 when the Scandinavian King Christian ran out of money. The Norse age in Scotland was over.

Timeline: The Vikings in Scotland

795 AD	First Viking raid on Iona
802 AD	Second raid on Iona
806 AD	Third raid on Iona with 68 monks killed
825 AD	St Blathmac murdered by Vikings
830 AD	Vikings settle on Orkney and Shetland
866 AD	Olaf of Dublin attacks Scotland on a hostage-taking raid
870 AD	Vikings attack Dumbarton
903 AD	Vikings attack Dunkeld in Perthshire
995 AD	Viking Earls of Orkney become Christian
1100 AD	Magnus Bareleg makes expedition to Scotland
1101 AD	Scottish King Edgar 'buys off' the Vikings
1200 AD	Scottish and Norwegian royal families inter-marry
1263 AD	Norwegian army perishes at 'Siege' of Largs
1266 AD	Norwegians lose control of the Hebrides
1472 AD	Scandinavian king loses control of Orkney and Shetland
1700 AD	Norse dialect of Norn dies out in northern islands

Things to Do

1. Read the Viking Timeline above and copy it into your jotter.
   Go to your class or school library and find out more about the events described in the timeline.

2. Use your school library to find out more about the following Viking topics: longships, sagas, Viking gods, Viking clothes, Viking trade routes. Plan and write a paragraph about each of these topics. Use illustrations in your reports.

Unit 3

The Coming of the Cross

3.1	How did Scotland become a Christian country?	26
3.2	What was different about the Celtic Church?	27
3.3	Who were Scotland's first great saints?	29
3.4	Who was the real Columba?	30
3.5	Why did St Andrew become the patron saint of Scotland?	31

3.1 How did Scotland become a Christian country?

THE EARLY tribes in Scotland were pagan. We know very little about their religion. There are many ancient circles in Scotland. They may have been used to worship the stars or the sun. The Picts may also have believed in water spirits.

After 400 AD the early peoples of Scotland were gradually converted to Christianity by a small group of brave men. They were missionaries from northern England and Ireland.

The first missionary was called Nynia or Ninian. We think he was the son of a Roman soldier who guarded Hadrian's Wall. As a young man he studied Latin and the Bible in Rome and at St Martin's monastery in France. Around the year 397 AD he was made a Bishop and was sent to spread the gospel in Northern Britain.

Ninian travelled to Galloway in south west Scotland with a small band of followers. They built a small stone church at Whithorn which was probably the first Christian church in Scotland. It was called the Candida Casa or White House. Later he travelled across to the north east to try and convert the Picts.

Source A: Early Christian cross from Whithorn in Galloway

Source B: An early Christian priest's cell, Firth of Lorn

The southern Picts gave up their pagan ways and accepted the true faith when the word of God was preached to them by Nynia, a most holy man and a Briton.

Source C: From an English chronicle written in 730 AD

The stone remains may be part of a wall belonging to the legendary Candida Casa which St Ninian is supposed to have built some time between 400 and 430 AD. Whithorn also contains a 5th century Latin tombstone and a very early Christian cemetery.

Source D: From a modern archaeological report on Whithorn

Things to Do

1. Why do you think missionaries like Ninian had to be brave?

2. How do Sources A, C and D suggest that Ninian successfully converted the people within his area?

3. (a) How would you describe the Christian building shown in Source B?
   (b) What does this building tell you about the life of an early priest?
   (c) What does it suggest about the wealth of the early Church?

3.2 What was different about the Celtic Church?

IN THE first centuries after Christ, people in different countries had their own ways of worshipping Him. By the year 600 AD, most western Europeans followed the traditions of the Roman Church. However, in Scotland, Northumbria and Ireland another form of Christianity had developed. This was the Celtic Church.

The Celtic and Roman Churches had many different customs, although in most cases this did not matter too much. They could not, however, agree on the correct date of Easter Sunday, the day of Christ's resurrection and the most important day in the Christian year. In 664 the powerful Northumbrian King Oswiu decided to follow the Roman date for Easter. Slowly the influence of Roman customs spread to Scotland and in 710 AD the Picts began to follow the rite of the Roman Catholic Church. The Celtic form of Christianity gradually faded away.

> AN ARGUMENT broke out over the date of Easter. The Queen of Northumbria kept the festival on the Roman date. When the King, who kept the Celtic date, had finished his Lenten fast and celebrated the Easter Risen Christ, the Queen was still fasting and preparing for Palm Sunday. It was agreed that a Synod be held at the monastery at Whitby. When the priests had finished speaking, King Oswiu of the Northumbrian asked, 'Which is greater in the kingdom of heaven, Columba or the Apostle Peter?' The whole synod replied with one voice, 'Thou art Peter and upon this rock I will build my church.' So King Oswiu followed the Roman Easter, for Peter was the foundation of the Roman Church.

Source A: From Bede's History of the Church, written in 730 AD

Things to Do

1. List the differences between the Celtic and Roman forms of Christianity described on pages 27 and 28.

2. According to Source A, why did King Oswiu eventually change to the Roman date for Easter? What do you think his real motives or reasons were for doing this?

3. Find out the meaning of the following words: synod, tonsure, apostle, abbot, bishop, cell, Mass, Lenten fast, Palm Sunday, monastery, gospel, rite, Pope.

4. Investigate the church buildings in your area. See if they use a Roman or Celtic form of Cross.

Source B: Roman (bottom) and Celtic (top) Crosses

Scotland in the Middle Ages 400 – 1450 AD

The Historian

Volume 1   Issue No. 2

Roman & Celtic Churches

Our Correspondent examines some of the differences between the Roman and Celtic churches.

ROMAN monks lived together in shared monastery buildings. They had a closed tonsure. Bishops were the important men in the Roman Church. They were appointed by the Pope for their ability. Churches were the most important buildings in the Roman form of Christianity. Roman monks spent most of their time praying and celebrating Mass.

CELTIC monks lived alone in bee-hive cells. They had an open tonsure. Abbots were the important men in the Celtic Church. They were chosen by the monks for their holiness. Monasteries were the most important buildings in the Celtic form of Christianity. Celtic monks spent most of their time preaching the gospel.

Roman and Celtic Tonsures

Roman Tonsure

In the years after 500 AD, Christian monks and priests began to shave the top of their heads. This shaving was called the tonsure. It was done to show everyone that they were clergy of the Christian faith. Some said it was also a reminder of the crown of thorns which Christ wore on the Cross. Roman monks wore a circular tonsure. Celtic monks shaved their hair to a different wedge-shaped design.

Celtic Tonsure

3.3 Who were Scotland's first great saints?

ST NINIAN was not the only missionary to bring the Christian message to Scotland. In the 590s, St Kentigern or Mungo worked amongst the pagan tribes in the Clyde valley. St Molouc founded a monastery at Lismore near Mull. Later, St Maelrubha took the gospel deep into the Highlands to Applecross in the far north west.

From the old written records, the chronicles, it seems that these missionaries had a hard time converting the Picts. The tribes in the north and east of Scotland were often happy with their old beliefs. However, the Christian message made a greater impact on the Scottish-Irish kingdom of Dalriata in Argyll. The Celtic Church was a great influence upon these early Scots. Many monks from Dalriata worked with Columba to found the great monastery of Iona in 563 AD.

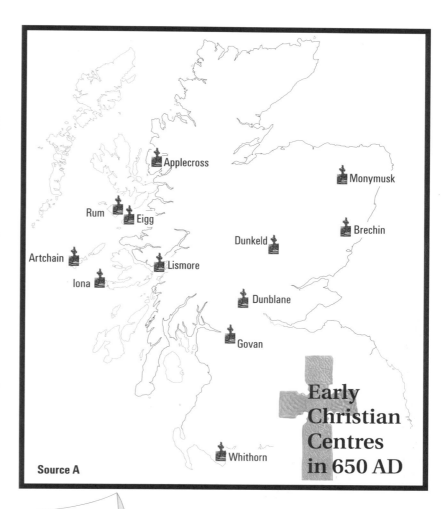

Source A

Early Christian Centres in 650 AD

Conthigurnus, or Kentigern meaning 'hound-lord', probably came from an aristocratic family in the Lothians. In the 590s he was bishop of a place called the 'green hollow' which may have been Glasgow. He probably looked more like an official or a prince than our modern idea of a monk. In the sixth century converting souls to Christ also meant winning new followers, land and prestige.

Source B: From a modern history book

Things to Do

1 Who were Scotland's first great saints?

2 Look at Source A and the information on this page. What do you notice about where the early Christian centres are located? What does this tell you about Christianity in Scotland at that time?

2 What reasons does Source B give to explain why the first missionaries were often from powerful families?

4 Using your school or public library, find out more about the early Christian centres nearest to your area.

3.4 Who was the real Columba?

COLUMBA was the first great saint of the Scots. His real name was Colum Cille which means 'Dove of the Church'. He is famous as a missionary who tried to convert the northern Picts to Christianity. He founded the great monastery on Iona in 563 AD.

We know a great deal about Columba because a book was written about him less than a hundred years after he died. It was written by Adamnan, an Abbot of Iona. Adamnan tells us that Columba was a very holy man who performed miracles and had visions of the future. He defeated the King of the Picts in a contest of magical powers. He even calmed a large monster that emerged from Loch Ness.

Modern historians have pieced together a very different picture of Columba. They believe he was an important Irish prince who was exiled to Dalriata for plotting a civil war. He was a leading Christian and he did try to spread the influence of the Celtic Church, but his real success was as a counsellor or adviser to the king of the Scots, Aedan.

Together they saved the small kingdom of Dalriata from attacks by the Picts, Britons and Angles.

> After Columba died his bones or relics were placed in a special box. This was the reliquary or Brecbannoch. It was the holiest object in medieval Scotland. The Scots believed it protected them and made their army invincible. More than 700 years after his death, the Scots carried the bones of Columba into the Battle of Bannockburn in 1314.

Source A: A modern historian

> Columba consecrated Aedan as King of Scots on Iona. For centuries, later kings of the Scots were buried together on this sacred isle.

Source B: From a modern history book

Source C: The Royal Cemetery on Iona

Things to Do

1. Why do you think Adamnan wrote a book about Columba? Do you think this book would be useful for historians?
2. Why should we be careful not to believe everything Adamnan tells us about Columba? What do you think Columba was really like?
3. Read Source A. What was the Brecbannoch? Why did the Scots carry it into battle?
4. According to Sources B and C, in what other ways was Iona a special place for the Scots?

Scotland in the Middle Ages 400 – 1450 AD

3.5 Why did St Andrew become the patron saint of Scotland?

THE NAME of St Kessog was the first war cry of the early Scottish army. The holy bones of St Columba were often carried into battle. However, by the year 1000 AD, Andrew, the fisherman from Galilee and the first Apostle, was the patron saint of Scotland. His shrine in north east Fife had taken over from Iona as the most important religious centre in the country. The Bishop of St Andrews gradually became the most powerful churchman in the kingdom.

In the 4th century a priest called Regulus fled from his home in Greece when it was attacked. He escaped by ship, taking with him the bodily remains of St Andrew. Regulus was shipwrecked on the coast of Scotland in Fife where he built a church to protect the relics of Christ's first follower.

Source A: The legend of St Regulus

King Angus II ruled from 726 to 761AD. The night before an important battle against the Angles, he dreamt that he saw the X shaped cross of St Andrew shining above his troops. Angus was victorious the next day and gave thanks to his saintly protector. From then on his army carried the flag of St Andrew.

Source B: A medieval legend

Source C: The flag or saltire of St Andrew

After 795 AD, Columba's shrine in the far west at Iona came under repeated attack from Viking sea raiders. The Scottish kings could no longer protect it. They probably decided to build a new religious centre nearer their main lands and forts in the east of Scotland. The great King Constantine II spent the last years of his life as a monk at the old church of Kilreymont in Fife. Over time it became the most important church in Scotland. Historians think that later kings allowed the legend of St Andrew to develop as it made Scotland seem more important to have one of Christ's apostles buried here. Kilreymont slowly became known as St Andrews.

Source D: A modern historian

Three fingers, a knee cap and a tooth of St Andrew were in the church at Hexham in Northumbria till Scottish raiders stole the bones in the year 960 and took them to Kilreymont in Fife. They placed them in an ancient church built by a Celtic saint called Riagail or Regulus in Latin.

Source E: From a 12th century chronicle

Things to Do

1. Why did Iona become less popular as a religious shrine?

2. In what ways were sources A and B used to strengthen St Andrew's links with Scotland?

3. Which of the accounts in the sources do you think is nearest to what really happened? Explain your choice.

Scotland in the Middle Ages 400 – 1450 AD

Unit 4

One Kingdom – Alba

4.1	What were the Kings of Alba like?	33
4.2	How did the MacAlpin Kings change Scotland?	35
4.3	Macbeth—Good King or Bad?	36
4.4	How was the Border decided?	37
4.5	Why was Canmore a new kind of King?	38
4.6	Why was Margaret made into a saint?	39
4.7	How did the common folk of Alba live?	40

4.1 What were the Kings of Alba like?

FROM the 840s onwards, the Picts and the Scots were ruled by the same kings. These kings spoke Gaelic and called their realm Alba. They were warrior kings who had to defend their territory from many enemies — Norsemen, Irish, Danes and English. Many of them died in battle.

Each new king of Alba was chosen by the leading men in the land. He had to be old enough and strong enough to fight to keep his power. Many of the Alban kings came from the dynasty or family of MacAlpin.

One of the greatest Alban kings was Constantine II who ruled from 903 to 943. This was a very long time for a Scottish king in those days. This fact alone tells us that he was an able ruler.

He lost as many battles as he won, but he strengthened the power of Alba. He did this through clever alliances and marriages with the Viking rulers of Dublin and York. Constantine pushed the boundary of his kingdom southwards into the Lothians. He was able to control the rebels and plotters amongst his own warriors who wanted to take his place as king. When he was an old man he abdicated, became a monk and died peacefully at St Andrews.

Source A: King Kenneth MacAlpin drawn in the 1600s

Scotland in the Middle Ages 400 – 1450 AD

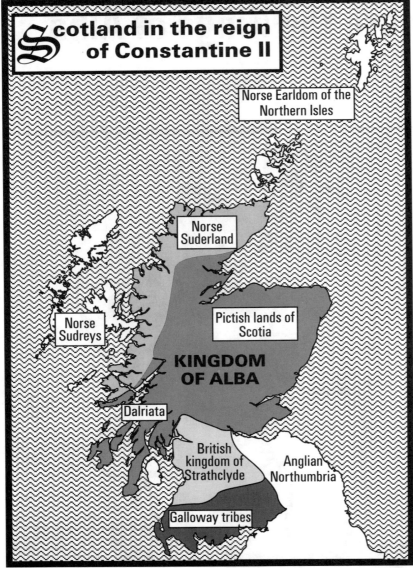

Source B

Things to Do

1. Why do you think the Kings of Alba were chosen, rather than succeeding from father to son?

2. What made Constantine II a 'good king'? Give at least three reasons in your answer.

3. Kenneth MacAlpin ruled from 843 to 858. The picture of him shown in Source A was drawn in the 1600s. Do you think he really looked like this? Explain your answer.

4. (a) Look at the list of Alban kings in Source C. How many of these kings only reigned for a few years?
   (b) What does this tell you about the job of being king of Scotland in those days?

5. Choose one of the kings on the list. Use your school or public library to find out more about him, then report back to your class.

Kenneth MacAlpin	843–858		Culen	966–971
Donald I	858–862		Kenneth II	971–975
Constantine I	862–877		Constantine III	995–997
Aed	877–878		Kenneth III	997–1005
Eochaid	878–889		Malcolm II	1005–1034
Donald II	889–900		Duncan I	1034–1040
Constantine II	903–943		Macbeth	1040–1057
Malcolm I	943–954	**KINGS OF ALBA**	Lulach	1057–1058
Indulf	954–962		Malcolm III	1058–1093
Dubh	962–966		Donald Bane	1093–1097

Source C

Scotland in the Middle Ages 400 – 1450 AD

4.2 How did the MacAlpin Kings change Scotland?

THE MacAlpin kings ruled from 843 to 1057. In that time Scotland changed in many ways:

- The old capital of Dalriata, Dunadd in Argyll, was abandoned. The kings moved to Perthshire, living in palace forts at Perth, Forteviot and Abernethy.

- Dunkeld and St Andrews in the east became the main religious centres of the kingdom, rather than Iona.

- Kings of Alba were consecrated or 'crowned' at Scone near Perth. The Stone of Destiny was taken to Scone for use in this ceremony.

- Much of modern southern Scotland was conquered at this time. Edinburgh became part of Alba in 962 and the Angles were slowly pushed southwards. The old British Kingdom of Strathclyde was also absorbed into Alba.

- The Scots of Alba slowly lost touch with their cousins in Ireland. The two peoples, once united by a similar language and culture, began to drift apart.

IN 906 King Constantine and his bishop Cellach of St Andrews pledged themselves upon the Hill of Faith near the royal city of Scone, that the laws and disciplines of the faith, and the rights in churches and gospels, should be kept in conformity with the customs of the Scots.

Source A: The consecration or 'coronation' of Constantine II

Source B: The Stone of Destiny — a replica held in the grounds of Scone Palace in Scotland

Things to Do

1. Use an atlas or map to find Dunadd, Scone, St Andrews, Forteviot, Abernethy, Dunkeld and Perth. Plot them on a blank map of Scotland with the heading *The Kingdom of Alba*.

2. Read Source A. Imagine you were on the Hill of Faith near Scone in 906. Write a short entry in your chronicle describing what took place, who was there, what you saw and why it was important.

3. Investigate the Stone of Destiny. Try to find out where it came from, why it was important to the Scots, and what happened to it.

4.3 Macbeth—Good King or Bad?

MACBETH is the most famous king of Alba nowadays. This is because the English playwright William Shakespeare wrote *The Tragedie of Macbeth* in 1605. This drama is still popular around the world almost four hundred years after it was first performed. Shakespeare's character of Macbeth is one of the most evil men in fiction—but what was the real King Macbeth like?

The Historian

Volume 1 — Issue No. 3

The real Macbeth

SOURCE A:
Macbeth according to Shakespeare in 1605

MACBETH is helped to power by three witches. His wife persuades Macbeth to murder the old King Duncan who is sleeping as a guest in Macbeth's castle. Duncan's guards are falsely blamed for the killing and are quickly executed by Macbeth. The Scottish royal family flees to England and Macbeth becomes king unlawfully.

He kills his best friend through jealousy. He murders the wife and children of one of his lords. The kingdom of Scotland is ruined while Macbeth is king. Macbeth and his wife become mad. She commits suicide. He is slain by Duncan's son and heir, Malcolm, who becomes the new lawful king.

SOURCE B:
Macbeth according to modern historians

THE real Macbeth was king of Alba between 1040 and 1057. For most of this time, Scotland was at peace. If he killed Duncan it was in a battle, not in bed. Duncan was a young man in his thirties.

Macbeth was a devout king. He visited Rome as a pilgrim in 1050 where he gave alms to the poor and offerings to the Church. Macbeth's wife, Queen Gruoch, gave land to monks who wanted to found a monastery at Loch Leven in Fife.

There is no mention of witches in the early records of Scotland, but they were a popular idea in the 1600s.

Macbeth lived in a wooden hall or palace. There were no stone castles in 11th century Scotland.

Macbeth did lose a battle against Malcolm in 1054 but lived on and ruled in his Moray homelands for another three years.

Macbeth meets the three witches according to Shakespeare.

Things to Do

1. Read Sources A and B carefully and think about them. How did Shakespeare try to make us think that Macbeth was an evil king? Why do you think he did this?

2. What do we know about the real Macbeth? In what ways was he different from Shakespeare's fictional king?

3. Shakespeare got some facts about Macbeth wrong. He did not know other things about him. We can now prove some of these errors. What are they?

4.4 How was the Border decided?

THE Alban kings led many expeditions to try and conquer southern Scotland. According to the chronicles, Kenneth MacAlpin crossed the Forth six times to fight the Angles in Lothian. Although the towns of Maelros and Dynbaer were sacked by the Scots, the kingdom of Alba was still limited to the lands north of the Forth-Clyde valley.

Many Alban kings tried to win control of the Lothians but failed. Then in 1018, King Malcolm II and his ally, King Owen of Strathclyde, joined forces. They met and destroyed the Anglian army at Carham near the River Tweed. Within weeks of this victory, Owen died and Malcolm's young grandson took his place. The lands of Strathclyde became part of Alba. Now almost all of North Britain had one king who was a Scot.

The kingdom of Alba was now strong enough to defend its new southern border along the River Tweed. It remains the dividing line between Scotland and England today. The English often attacked Scotland again, but they were never able to occupy it for any length of time.

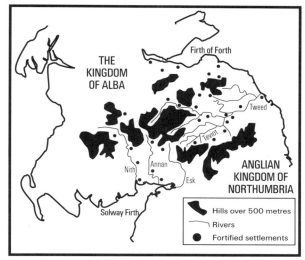

Source A: The Border defences

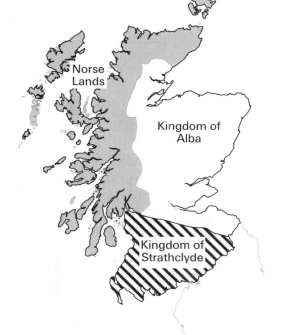

Source B: Alba in the year 1000 AD

Source C: A modern historian

Things to Do

1. Why do you think the kings of Alba wanted to control the Lothians?

2. Look at Source A. What natural features helped the Scots to defend the border with England? How did the Scots strengthen the border?

3. Explain the view of the historian in Source C, giving at least two reasons to support his statement.

4. What are Maelros and Dynbaer called today? Find them on a map of Scotland.

Scotland in the Middle Ages 400 – 1450 AD

4.5 Why was Canmore a new kind of King?

MACBETH was the last of the old kings of Alba. His place was taken by Malcolm III Canmore in 1058. Canmore was a Gaelic title which meant 'Great Head' or 'Chieftain'. However, Malcolm had grown up in Northumbria and so he also spoke English and French.

Canmore moved his capital from the old Pictish places in Perthshire. He spent most of his time in the Lowlands where the people had mixed with the Angles and spoke their southern tongue. In 1070 he married Margaret, a princess brought up in the English court. Their children, Edward, Edgar, Edmund and Edith, were given English, not Gaelic, names.

Malcolm copied something else from the English. At Dunfermline he built a new kind of stronghold, called King Malcolm's Tower. It was probably the first castle in the kingdom. He also spent much of his time on the fortifications of Din Eidyn, or Edinburgh as it was called in English.

Source A: King Malcolm's Tower, Dunfermline

Many of the old Celtic nobles and earls distrusted the new southern customs which Malcolm had learned in England. When Malcolm died, they passed over his English speaking sons. Instead they chose a Gaelic prince, Donald Bain, as the next king. Probably he had promised to rule in the traditional ways.

Source B: From a modern history book

Things to Do

1. (a) What do you think the castle in Source A made from? How was it different from the castles which you can see today?
   (b) Very little of the original King Malcolm's Tower survives today. Can you suggest a reason for this?

2. Why do you think Malcolm spent much of his time in his castles?

3. Why do some historians think that he was not a very popular king in some parts of Scotland?

Scotland in the Middle Ages 400 – 1450 AD

4.6 Why was Margaret made into a saint?

MARGARET became Queen of Scotland in 1070. She was an intelligent and very religious woman who had been educated in Europe and England. Determined to modernise Scotland, she introduced many of the new ideas she had seen in the richer towns and castles of England and the Continent.

 She made Sunday into a day of worship and banned the old Celtic custom of holding markets and festivals on that day.

 She invited Benedictine monks from England to build a monastery at Dunfermline. They were men with new ideas and skills in farming and building which Scotland needed.

 She built a small chapel in Edinburgh Castle in the new modern Norman style. It survives today and is the oldest standing church in Scotland.

 She gave large sums of money and grants of land to the Church to help the poor.

 She made it easier for pilgrims to cross the River Forth so that they could visit the holy shrine of St Andrew in Fife.

Margaret did kind acts partly because she knew it was important for the monarchy to keep the loyalty of the common people. She also knew that acts of charity could be turned into rituals or ceremonies where the power and generosity of the king and queen were put on public display.

Source A: The view of a modern historian

Source B: The coat of arms of South Queensferry

MARGARET was the most holy woman to have lived in Scotland. She spent hours each day in her chapel at prayer. She did many kind acts of charity. She was a saint.

Source C: The view of Turgot, Margaret's priest and friend.

Things to Do

1. Compare Sources A and C. With a friend, discuss the reasons why Margaret was kind to the poor. Which of the two writers is the more believable? Give your reasons for thinking this.

2. Look at Source B. Investigate the history of Queensferry. Find out how Margaret helped pilgrims to get to St Andrews.

3. (a) Copy and colour the South Queensferry coat of arms.
   (b) Use your information about Queen Margaret to explain the different parts of this coat of arms.

Scotland in the Middle Ages 400 – 1450 AD

4.7 How did the commonfolk of Alba live?

Source A: A clachan

THERE WERE still very few people living in Alba in 1000 AD. There were probably less than half a million Scots at this time. They lived in an empty land where there was a great deal of wilderness in which to hunt. There were many farms in southern Scotland, but there was still enough forest to provide other sources of food in a year when the harvest was poor. Timber and peat could easily be found to burn as fuel.

No real towns existed. Most families lived in small villages, later called clachans in Gaelic or touns in English. The farmers in these clachans kept sheep and some cattle and we know that they grew crops in some areas. Historians think the land in these clachans was shared out by the community, rather than being owned by any one man or family.

In dangerous times, these farm villagers often needed protection. They got this from the Mormaers. These were powerful armed chieftains who ruled large districts in Moray, Angus and Argyll. The folk in the touns paid a food rent of corn, cheese and cattle to these chiefs and warriors in exchange for safety.

Things to Do

1. Look at Source A.
   (a) How many ways of getting food can you see in this clachan?
   (b) Do you think the people of Alba were well fed?
   (c) What do you think life was like in a clachan?
   (d) What might these people have lacked in their lives?

Scotland in the Middle Ages 400 – 1450 AD

Unit 5

The Normans in Scotland

5.1	Who were the Normans?	42
5.2	Why did the Normans come to Scotland	43
5.3	What was a motte and bailey castle?	44
5.4	Why did the Normans build castles on their estates?	45
5.5	What was feudalism?	46
5.6	How did the Normans change the government of Scotland?	47
5.7	Why was David I a great King?	48

5.1 Who were the Normans?

THE FIRST Normans were Vikings or Norsemen who attacked France in 885 AD. They sailed up the River Seine in their longships and besieged Paris. Many of the Norsemen decided to settle on the rich farmlands of northern France. In 910 they were given a large piece of land by the French king. This became known as the Dukedom of Normandy. In time, the Normans mixed with the local French population. They gave up their old pagan ways and became Christian. By 1000 AD they even spoke a kind of French.

The Normans were a powerful, well-organised people. They encouraged the growth of both trade and towns in their dukedom. In these towns they built many churches and abbeys. They had a strong army of full-time soldiers or knights who practised the skills of war. These knights wore armour and fought on horseback, held in place by a new invention called the stirrup. They also defended themselves by building strongholds or castles.

After 1000 AD the Normans began to spread out from their dukedom in France. They conquered Sicily and southern Italy and set up Norman kingdoms there. In other parts of Europe they were often given land and titles in exchange for their services as soldiers. Wherever they settled, the Normans built things in their own style and influenced the local population.

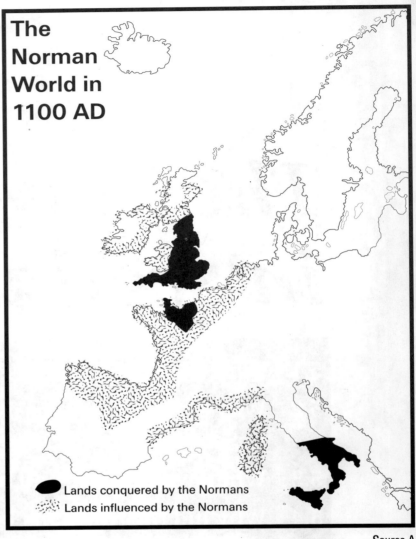

Source A

Things to Do

1. (a) Why do you think the first Normans attacked France?
   (b) Why do you think they were given land by the French king?

2. How were the first Normans changed by living in France?

3. Look at Source A. Make a list of the places which the Normans conquered.
   Make a second list of the places which they influenced.

5.2 Why did the Normans come to Scotland?

IN 1066 the Normans won their greatest prize. An army of Norman knights landed at Hastings on the south coast of England. The Normans destroyed the English army, killed the English king and marched on London. Duke William of Normandy was crowned king of England in Westminster Abbey. The Normans had captured one of the richest kingdoms in Europe.

This was a problem for the Scots. The Normans were very powerful and dangerous neighbours. They invaded Scotland in 1071 with a huge army and fleet. To avoid certain defeat, the Scottish king, Malcolm III, had to pay homage to the Normans. His sons, Edgar, Alexander and David realised that they could learn a great deal from these successful newcomers. From that time on, these English or Anglo-Normans had a great deal of influence in Scotland:

- Norman troops were sent by the English to decide who would be the next king of Scotland in 1097.
- After 1100 many Norman knights were invited to come into Scotland and were given land. In exchange they promised to fight for the Scottish king.
- Across southern Scotland, local people were forced to build wooden and earth-walled forts for the new Norman lords.
- Norman knights were given important jobs in the government of the kingdom, such as being sheriffs and justiciars.
- The Normans brought many new ideas from France into Scotland which helped to change our Church, law and language.

Things to Do

1. Explain why the Norman conquest of England was a problem for the Scots.
2. (a) Why do you think Scottish kings invited Norman knights to come and stay in Scotland?
   (b) Why were they mostly given land in southern Scotland?
   (c) Suggest a reason why Scotland was never conquered by the Normans.
3. How was Scotland changed by the coming of the Normans?
   Why do you think the kings of Scotland admired the Normans and copied their way of doing things?
4. Look at the list of names in Source B. What do you notice about them?
   What does this tell you about the Norman influence on Scotland?
5. Use your class or school library to find out why the style of building in Source A is called Norman. Which parts of the church tell you that it was built by Normans?

Source A: Norman church at Leuchars in Fife

Names of Norman knights who came to Scotland

Stewart
de Brus or Bruce
de Wallys or Wallace
Lindsay
Corbet
Grant
Fraser
de Mesnieres or Menzies
de Comyn or Cumming
Agnew
Sinclair
Berkeley or Barclay
Montgomery
Ramsay
Bisset
Gourlay
Beaton

Source B

Scotland in the Middle Ages 400 – 1450 AD

5.3 What was a motte and bailey castle?

MANY Norman soldiers were given grants of land or estates by the Scottish king. The first thing these new Norman lords did was to build a motte and bailey castle on their estates. A mound of earth was quickly raised up, making the motte or hill. A wooden stockade or fence was built around the top of the motte. Inside this, a wooden tower was built as a safe place and a look-out for the Norman troops. Around the bottom of the motte was a second outer wall which encircled the bailey or courtyard. In the bailey there were usually stables, kitchens, barns and a chapel. Some motte and bailey castles had ditches around the bailey wall which gave extra protection.

Often the local people were forced to build a motte and bailey castle for their new Norman master. In time, these simple wooden and earth forts were replaced with much stronger stone castles.

Because these early Norman forts were made of timber, only the earthworks on which they stood remain today. The wooden buildings have rotted away.

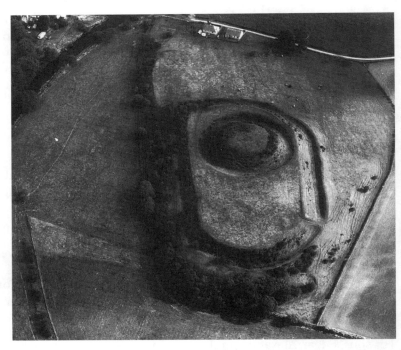

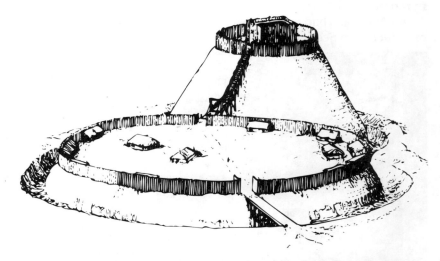

Source A: Above, the Motte of Urr, Stewartry, seen from the air. Below, an artist's impression of the site.

Things to Do

1. (a) Why were the first castles in Scotland made of wood and earth?
   (b) What would be the advantages and disadvantages of building a castle in this way?

2. Look at Source A. Why do you think this site was chosen for a castle?

3. If no motte and bailey castles survive today, how do you think we know what they looked like?

5.4 Why did the Normans build castles on their estates?

THE NORMANS built strong stone castles so that they could control the surrounding countryside. They could ride out with their troops to collect rent and food from the local population. Inside the castle they were safe from attack. Often the Norman knights were away at war, so they needed somewhere safe to store their goods and protect their families. Some Anglo-Normans were deliberately given land in important places. Their castles were close to river crossings, bridges, roads or natural harbours. They could hold these safe for the king and charge a toll or fee.

The Normans were not welcomed by everyone in Scotland. They were foreigners who spoke French. They were also powerful men who wanted to change the way Scotland was governed. There were many people in Scotland who feared and disliked the Norman newcomers. Many Scots preferred the old Celtic ways of life. There were several local rebellions against the Norman knights, especially by the proud tribes of Galloway.

King Malcolm III and his wife Queen Margaret admired the Normans, but when they died in 1093 they were succeeded by a Gaelic prince from the Hebrides called Donald Bain. Four years of war broke out between the Anglo-Normans and those Northern Scots who wanted to expel the newcomers from the kingdom. Donald Bain was defeated, blinded and imprisoned in 1097 by a Norman force from southern Scotland and England. A younger son of Margaret, called Edgar, became king of Scotland, but he depended on the swords of his Norman allies.

Source A: Caerlaverock Castle, near Dumfries, in 1300 AD

Things to Do

1. Copy the page heading into your jotter. Write out and explain as many reasons as you can which help to answer the question.

2. (a) Why do you think Donald Bain wanted to expel the Normans from Scotland?
   (b) What was the outcome of his actions?

3. Look at Source A. Why is this a good place to build a castle?
   Write down two things which the lord of the castle could control.

Scotland in the Middle Ages 400 – 1450 AD

5.5 What was feudalism?

IN THE DAYS of Alba there were families of Gaelic princes who ran large parts of the country. They were princes because they were sons of great chiefs and because they could muster large bands of warriors in times of trouble. In peacetime the princes lived with the local people in their tribal homelands. Often the kings of Alba found it difficult to control these Celtic chieftains.

The Normans brought a new way of running the country to Scotland. This was called *feudalism*. The Normans brought feudalism from France to England and into Scotland. When Scotland became a feudal kingdom, all the land was said to be owned by the king. He granted large pieces of land or estates to his most trusted followers, who were often Norman barons. In return they promised to be loyal to the king, and to fight for him in war.

The barons also granted some of the land on their estates to their most loyal troops or knights in return for military service. Under the knights were the free tenant farmers who worked the land and paid their rent in food and other produce which they gave to their lord. Each man depended on his lord for land and protection. Each man owed his lord obedience, loyalty and service. Sometimes an abbey or a burgh took the place of an actual lord.

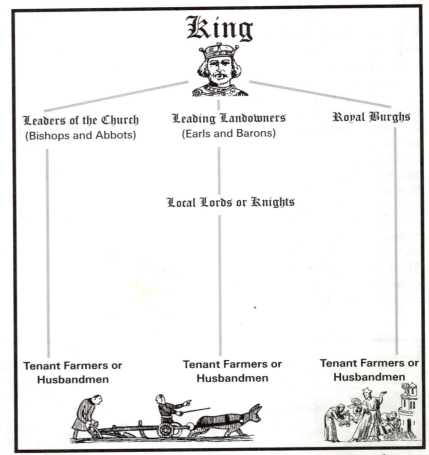

Source A: The feudal system

> The old Gaelic aristocracy protected and favoured their kin, people with whom they had a blood relationship. In the new feudal system any man could swear fealty or allegiance to a lord. He paid homage by placing his hands within those of his lord and promising to be his man (or homme in Norman French). Each knight was meant to receive a feu or fief, a piece of land large enough to provide the money to feed and equip a knight and his horse.

Source B: From a modern history book

Things to Do

1. Copy the diagram in Source A into your jotter.

2. Write out the meaning of the following words: estate, baron, knight, feu, fealty, homage, tenant. Work out the meanings from the text above and from Source B.

3. Explain why the kings of Scotland preferred feudalism to the old ways of running the country. Try and give at least three reasons why this was.

5.6 How did the Normans change the Government of Scotland?

THE OLD KINGS of Alba had moved around the country with bands of armed followers. They expected to be fed and entertained by the local chiefs and princes. They had no fixed capital town, although they spent the winters in a safe fortress. When they were not at war, the kings spent much of their time hunting or feasting.

Between 1097 and 1153 the kings of Scotland were brothers, Edgar, Alexander I and David I. They are sometimes called Normanisers, because they copied many new ideas from England and France. Edgar chose to settle at Edinburgh Castle which became the centre of his kingdom. This was where the king held his Court. He was helped by new officials who had French names and who became the most important men in Scotland after the king.

The Chancellor kept the records of those who had been granted land or privileges by the king. He was in charge of the king's seal which was used to stamp letters and charters to make them official. The Constable policed the Castle and was in charge of the king's guard. The Steward was in charge of daily life in the castle household. It was his job to oversee the servants in the kitchens and the royal chambers. The Chamberlain guarded the king's money chest. He made sure that rents and taxes were paid to the king.

Source A: The seal of King David I

Things to Do

1. How did the government of Scotland change under the Normanisers?

2. Why do you think the new Court officials became the most important men in the kingdom?

3. Which of the Court officials was the most important? Give a reason for your answer.

4. Look at Source A. Why were seals like this important? What did they prove?

Scotland in the Middle Ages 400 – 1450 AD

5.7 Why was David I a Great King?

DAVID I RULED Scotland from 1124 to 1153. Before he became King of Scotland, he lived in England where he had large estates. He was the greatest of the Normanisers:

♛ He founded many of Scotland's most important towns. These were the King's Burghs. Traders who lived in these burghs were given special rights and privileges.

♛ He minted Scotland's first silver coins to encourage trade and commerce. Before this, most Scots exchanged goods by barter.

♛ He ordered fairs to be held in the largest towns. These fairs attracted merchants and their goods to Scotland from England and other parts of Europe.

♛ He extended the amount of land under royal control. These new lands were held by trusted knights who were allowed to build their own castles.

♛ He used his Norman troops to put down any rebellions against his rule, such as the rising of the Moray men in 1130.

♛ Although he lost a major battle against the English in 1138, he captured the wealthy town of Carlisle in Northern England.

♛ He ended the quarrel between the Roman and Celtic Churches. He helped the building of abbeys at Melrose and Kinloss. He used leading churchmen as government advisers and officials.

♛ He ruled for nearly thirty years, a long time in the Middle Ages. During his reign Scotland became a stronger, more unified country.

♛ For nearly 150 years after his death, Scotland was at peace and grew in prosperity.

Source A: From a modern History book

> The Gaelic kings were tribal chieftains writ large. The Normanisers were administrators who wanted to build up a strong, centralised kingdom that was prosperous enough to compete with its powerful neighbours.

Source B

Things to Do

1. What actions did David take to make Scotland prosperous?

2. Read Source A. Discuss it with a friend. Read through Unit 5, then say whether you agree with the writer of Source A or not. Use the information in Unit 5 to argue your point of view.

3. Look at Source B. Choose one of the King's Burghs. Use your school library to find out more about its history. See if you can find out why David chose to build a burgh on that site.

4. Research the life of King David I. Write a short report on him with the following title:

   Why was David one of the great kings of Scotland?

Scotland in the Middle Ages 400 – 1450 AD

Unit 6

In Time of War

6.1	Where were Scotland's castles built?	50
6.2	How successful was the Scottish army?	51
6.3	Who were the Sheriffs?	53
6.4	What was a wapinschaw?	54
6.5	Were Scottish towns and castles ever beseiged?	55
6.6	What was a Tower House?	57

6.1 Where were Scotland's castles built?

Source A: The fortress of Dumbarton Rock

THE FIRST CASTLES in Scotland were built by the new Norman lords. Others were built by Scottish lords from older Alban families who copied the new ideas from France and England. These were motte and bailey castles made of earth and wood with stockades. They were built quickly, usually in the middle of the lands granted to the lord. He wanted somewhere that was safe from attack. It also had to be somewhere easy for his farmers and peasants to reach in times of trouble.

The three royal fortresses of Edinburgh, Stirling and Dumbarton were built on rocky volcanic sites which were difficult to capture. Some castles, like Hermitage in the Borders, were built in marshy areas that were difficult to penetrate. Many later stone castles were built to control a road, a pass through the hills, a harbour or a river crossing.

Often castles were linked in some way. Tantallon and Craigmillar in the Lothians were part of a chain of fortresses, towers and beacons that protected southern Scotland from English invasion. Dozens of towers and mottes were built by the Scots in the 1160s and 1170s to police the wild tribes of Galloway. Many castles in the west, such as Dunstaffnage near Oban, were built to keep control of land won back from the Norse kings.

> THE Gallwegians treacherously made a conspiracy and separated themselves from the kingdom of Scotland. They expelled from all of Galloway the bailiffs, guards and other officials which the king of Scots had set over them and they besieged, captured and destroyed all the towers and castles which the king of Scots had built in their land for the keeping of good order there.
>
> **Source B:** From a Scottish chronicle for 1174

Things to Do

1. How did lords in medieval Scotland decide where to build their castles?

2. (a) Why were many castles built in Galloway after 1160?
   (b) According to Source B, how successful were the Scots in controlling Galloway?

3. Why was Dumbarton Rock an especially good site for a royal castle?

6.2 How successful was the Scottish army?

BETWEEN 1296 and 1450 Scotland was often at war with England. The English invaded Scotland several times and captured many of the southern towns and castles. Scottish kings often raided the northern English counties and sometimes sent armies to fight the English in Ireland and France.

The English almost always had larger forces. Their army was mostly made up of professional soldiers who were paid for their skill at fighting. Many of these knights and men-at-arms were excellent warriors who had trained in the arts of war. The Scottish army was usually smaller and was made up of part-time soldiers. They performed a service called 'forinsec', agreeing to follow their lord to war for 40 days. Most Scottish troops were peasants and farmers who were keen to get back to their crops and animals as soon as they could.

The Scots suffered several terrible defeats when they met the English in open battle. Their army was destroyed in battles such as Falkirk in 1298, Dupplin in 1332, Halidon Hill in 1333, Neville's Cross in 1346, and Homildon in 1402. However, the English found it difficult to conquer the Scots who fought back in a number of ways:

- The Scots 'scorched the earth' of southern Scotland, leaving no crops or animals for the invading English army to eat.
- They lured the English into slow, expensive sieges at the royal fortresses of Stirling and Edinburgh which were well garrisoned and difficult to capture.
- The Scots destroyed their own castles so that they could not be used by the English.
- The Scots retreated northwards over the Tay and the Clyde until they were strong enough to hit back at their enemy.
- They harassed the English, cutting off their communication and supply lines, and hoping that hunger, disease or a cold winter would make them turn back.

> THE Scots are bold, hardy and much used to war...they march from twenty to twenty four leagues without halting, by night as well as day. They bring no carriages with them nor do they carry any stores of bread or wine for they will live for a long time on meat half sodden, without bread, and drink the river water without wine...Each man carries a little bag of oatmeal; when they have eaten too much of the sodden meat and their stomachs appear weak and empty, they place their plate over the fire, mix the oatmeal with water and make a thin cake like a cracknel or biscuit, which they eat to warm their stomachs; it is therefore no wonder that they perform a longer day's march than other soldiers.
>
> **Source A:** From a French 14th century chronicle

> Compared to the professional English and French armies, the Scots were an ill-armed, poorly trained assortment of peasants with a sprinkling of feudal knights. At times they must have seemed like a rabble to the skilled English men-at-arms.

Source B: A modern historian in 1977

Scotland in the Middle Ages 400 – 1450 AD

Source C: A modern historian writing in 1991

Things to Do

1. (a) What was forinsec?
   (b) In what ways were the Scottish and English armies different?

2. (a) What do you think is meant by open battle?
   (b) Why do you think the Scots lost most of their battles against the English?
   (c) Why were the English unable to use their strength to conquer Scotland?

3. The writer of Source A thought that the Scots were good soldiers. In your own words give at least two reasons why this was his opinion.

4. Read Sources B and C. Write a paragraph explaining the different points of view of these two writers, then say which of them you agree with. Use the evidence on page 51 to back up your choice.

5. Pick one of the battles mentioned in the text. Find out where and why it was fought. Find out why it was lost by the Scots.

6.3 Who were the Sheriffs?

THE SHERIFFS were important nobles who served as officials for the king. They kept the main royal castles in good repair and ready for war. They also looked after the royal estates, the large pieces of land which the king kept for himself. The first five sheriffs in Scotland were appointed by David I. They were put in charge of the important royal fortresses at Edinburgh, Stirling, Lanark, Berwick and Roxburgh.

Each sheriff was put in charge of a part of the kingdom which was called a shire. The sheriff had to collect rent and taxes from the farmers and smaller landowners in the shire, and also from the merchants and traders in the growing towns. He had to make sure that the royal stores were kept filled, in case the king took up residence or in case of a siege in wartime. It was the sheriff's duty to raise a garrison of troops to defend the royal castle. He also made sure that the shire sent the right number of troops to fight in the king's army.

When the king was not in the shire, the sheriff had to keep law and order. He sat as judge in the Great Hall hearing cases. He could fine or imprison the guilty. Sheriffs had to keep accurate records of how they did their job so that they could explain their actions to the king.

Expenses for 1266

For the hire of a crossbowman	2 merks and a half
For the food and service of two watchmen	20 shillings
For the food and service of a gatekeeper	8 shillings
For repairing the buildings of the castle of Ayr	27 shillings
The expenses of scouts spying on the king of Norway	24 shillings and 8 pence
To four men for watching the king's ships for 23 weeks	16 shillings and 10 pence
Three dozen staves bought for the use of crossbowmen	13 shillings and 4 pence
Salt bought for the provisioning of the castle	20 shillings
Ten chalders of oats for provisioning the castle	10 pounds
Six chalders of corn for provisioning the castle	9 pounds and 3 shillings

Source A: From the records of William, Sheriff of Ayr, 1266

Things to Do

1. Why would the sheriffs have to be trusted friends of the king?

2. Suggest a reason why modern historians know a lot about the work of the sheriffs.

3. Look at Source A. What does this source tell you about the work of a sheriff? What does it tell you about life in Ayr Castle in 1266?

4. Use your school library to investigate the meaning of the word sheriff.

6.4 What was a wapinschaw?

THERE WERE very few paid soldiers in the Scottish army in the Middle Ages. Each local lord had to promise that he would bring troops to the king's aid when they were needed. All husbandmen or farmers who owned goods worth £10 had to be ready to fight when the country was invaded. Most Scottish troops were 'humble or ordinary men' who fought as infantry or footsoldiers. The lords fought on horseback as mounted knights but they were always fewer in number.

In 1318 the Scottish Parliament passed a law which said that each soldier had to have his own weapons and know how to use them. A wapinschaw, or weaponshowing, was an inspection to check that the law was carried out. The wapinschaw was usually run by the sheriff or a local baron and normally took place twice a year. Every man between the ages of 16 and 60 promised his lord that he would follow him to war for up to 40 days each year. If the Scots were going raiding in England, only the best men were needed. They were chosen at the wapinschaw.

The Scottish Parliament also passed laws trying to ban football and golf. It wanted the men of Scotland to use their leisure time practising their skills with spear and bow instead.

Source A: Scottish soldiers in 1314

> IT IS ordanyt that in the tym of were ilk lawyt man of the kynrik that hes x lib. in gudis sal haf for his body in the defence of the kynrik a gud and suffyciand acton, a basnet, and gluffis of playt with a sper and a suerd... And the kyng wills that evir ilk schiref of the kynrik wyth the lordis of the placis inquer apon their thyngis and thai sal mak wapynschawyn. Alsua the kyng willis that ilk man hafand in gudis the valour of a kow sal haf a gud sper or a gud bow wyth a schaff of arowys that is to say xxiiii arowys...
>
> (ilk=each; kynrik=kingdom; acton=leather jacket; basnet=stell helmet)

Source B: The Scottish military law in 1318

Things to Do

1. Source B is written in medieval Scots. With a friend, read it out carefully and try to translate it into modern English. Then answer the questions below:
   (a) What weapons did Scotsmen have to provide?
   (b) Who checked that the law was carried out?

2. Source A is a modern picture. From what you have read about medieval Scottish soldiers on this page, how accurate do you think it is? Give reasons to support your opinion.

6.5 Were Scottish towns and castles ever besieged?

A SIEGE TOOK place when a town or a castle refused to surrender to an enemy army. The attackers would try to break through the walls, tunnel under the defences, or starve the defenders. According to the medieval laws of war, a besieged town or castle could be given a chance to surrender peacefully. If the defenders refused this offer, the town could be sacked or looted and the inhabitants slaughtered.

Usually the Scots were happy to let the English besiege their strong-points. Sieges were slow, expensive and often unsuccessful. They tied the English army down to one place. If the siege lasted long enough, winter and sickness could help to destroy the English forces.

The rich trading city of Berwick was Scotland's main port before 1300. In 1296 the English king, Edward I, besieged Berwick and sacked it. People throughout Scotland and Europe were horrified when they heard the terrible news of Edward's cruelty. The sack of Berwick was one of the events which made many Scots reject Edward as their overlord.

In 1306 a great siege took place at the massive stone castle of Kildrummy. The castle was held by the Bruce family and was one of the strongest in the kingdom. The English used siege machines to try and take the fortress, but it was only captured through an act of treachery. An English sympathiser set fire to the grain store inside the castle. The defenders were executed and the castle was dismantled.

Source A: A siege in the fourteenth century

Sometimes fortresses were taken peacefully. Defenders would agree to surrender a castle or a town if no reinforcements arrived by a certain date. In 1313 the Scots made an agreement like this with Lord Moubray, the English governor at Stirling Castle. He was to leave Stirling with his troops if no English army arrived to reinforce him by Midsummer of 1314. This agreement led to the Battle of Bannockburn.

Scotland in the Middle Ages 400 – 1450 AD

The Historian

Volume 1 Issue No.4

The Sack of Berwick

Source B: This source is taken from from a medieval chronicle

EDWARD with a large force came upon the town of Berwick. As he could not take it by force, he thought to outwit the garrison by sleight and cunning. So he pretended he was going to withdraw and, striking his tents, he made a feint of going far away. But on the 30th March, bearing aloft craftily counterfeited banners and war-ensigns of the Scottish army, he neared the gates of the town. When the Scots garrison saw this, they became right glad and merry, because they had got news that their king would soon be there to rescue and help them; and being thus unhappily deceived through that promise, they trustfully opened their gates, like true men that knew no guile. But as soon as the trick was found out and they became aware of the truth, they strove to withstand the foe. However, being hemmed in by the enemy, and assaulted on every side, they were wretchedly borne down. In this way the town was taken and all were swept down, and sparing neither sex nor age, the King of England in his tyrannous rage put to the sword 7500 souls of both sexes, so that for two days streams of blood flowed from the bodies of the slain.

Things to Do

1. Look at the evidence in the Sources and text above. List the ways in which castles and towns in Scotland were often captured.

2. Read Sources B carefully. How was the city of Berwick captured? Why do you think people felt that the Sack of Berwick was particularly cruel? Why did some people say that it was against the rules of war?

3. How has the writer of Source B tried to make sure that his readers form a poor opinion of the English King Edward? How does he describe the Scots defenders of Berwick?

4. How did the events at Berwick in 1296 affect the way the Scots felt about King Edward and the English?

5. Investigate the history of a castle or town in your part of Scotland. Find out if it was ever besieged. Was it captured or was it defended successfully?

The Sack of Berwick in 1296 was a key event in the growth of a Scottish sense of separateness from England.

Source C: A modern historian

6.6 What was a Tower House?

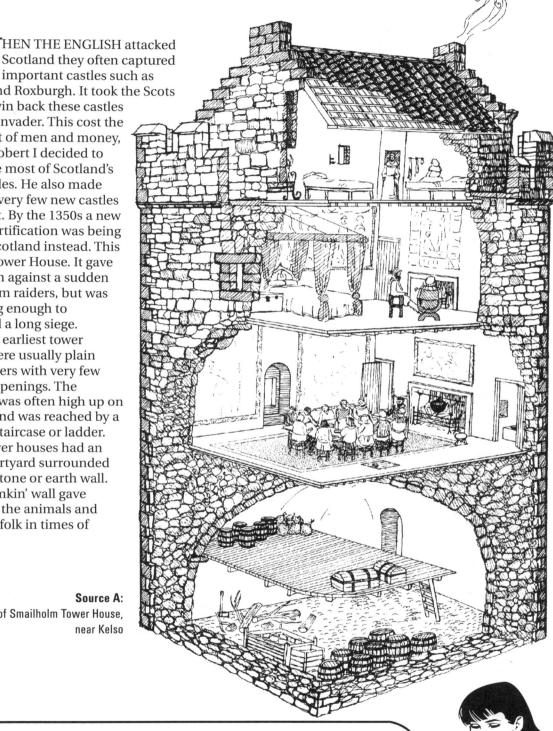

WHEN THE ENGLISH attacked Scotland they often captured important castles such as Stirling and Roxburgh. It took the Scots years to win back these castles from the invader. This cost the Scots a lot of men and money, so King Robert I decided to dismantle most of Scotland's large castles. He also made sure that very few new castles were built. By the 1350s a new kind of fortification was being built in Scotland instead. This was the Tower House. It gave protection against a sudden attack from raiders, but was not strong enough to withstand a long siege.

The earliest tower houses were usually plain stone towers with very few window openings. The entrance was often high up on the wall and was reached by a wooden staircase or ladder. Many tower houses had an outer courtyard surrounded by a low stone or earth wall. This 'barmkin' wall gave shelter to the animals and common folk in times of trouble.

Source A: Plan of Smailholm Tower House, near Kelso

> The tower house developed because of royal policy. The government in Edinburgh discouraged the building of large castles after 1330. The bitter experience of the wars with England had taught the lesson that Scotland's great castles could be used against Scotland's king. From now on, the local barons were to be housed in fortifications that could not hold out against the royal army.
>
> **Source B:** A modern historian

Scotland in the Middle Ages 400 – 1450 AD

Source C: A modern historian

> IN those days there was no law in Scotland; but the great man oppressed the poor man and the whole country was a den of thieves. Slaughters, robberies, fire-raising and other crimes went unpunished, and justice was banished beyond the kingdom's bounds.

Source D: One writer's opinion of Scotland from a chronicle written in 1400

Source E: Borthwick Castle in Midlothian

Source F: Craigievar in Aberdeenshire

Things to Do

1. (a) Look at Source A. List the things which make this tower house difficult to capture.
   (b) In what way was a tower house different from earlier castles?

2. (a) According to the text, why did King Robert allow his barons to build only tower houses?
   (b) For what reasons were tower houses needed, according to the writer of Source D?

3. Read Sources B and C. What different reasons do they give to explain the development of tower houses? Which historian do you believe more? Explain why.

4. Look at Source A. Why do you think the lower part of the tower house was used for storing goods? Why were the living quarters on the higher floors?

5. Compare the fortified houses in Sources E and F. What differences do you see?

Scotland in the Middle Ages 400 – 1450 AD

Unit 7

The Medieval Church

7.1	Why was the Church important in medieval Scotland?	60
7.2	What was a parish church like?	61
7.3	Why was St Andrews Cathedral a wealthy church?	62
7.4	Why were the monastic orders important for Scotland?	64
7.5	Why did monasteries and abbeys flourish in Scotland?	65
7.6	Who were the Friars?	66
7.7	Why did the Church run the schools in medieval Scotland?	68
7.8	Why did many Scots have to study in Europe	69

7.1 Why was the Church important in medieval Scotland?

RELIGION WAS a very important part of daily life in medieval Scotland. Everyone believed in God and the Devil. Everyone believed in heaven and hell. Every Scot was a Christian and a member of the Roman Catholic Church. This was the Church to which all western Europeans belonged. Its leader was the Bishop of Rome or the Pope. As Christ's vicar on earth, the Pope was the most important ruler in Christendom.

For much of the Middle Ages, the Church helped to run the kingdom. The best educated people in Scotland were priests, so churchmen like the Bishops of Glasgow and St Andrews helped the king to manage the country. The Church was in charge of the schools and it educated the young. It also owned the hospitals where the sick and aged were cared for.

The poor looked to the Church for alms or financial help.

All Scots had to attend church regularly and obey its laws. If they did not do so, they could be taken to a church court, tried and fined. The Church was also a big land-owner with large estates in Scotland. Many farmers and peasants lived and worked on Church land. They owed their livelihood to the Church, so they obeyed the local Church leaders.

Source A: A medieval church painting of Hell

Source B: A modern historian

Speech bubble: The Church was of great importance to people in medieval Scotland. It also influenced the daily lives of medieval Scots, and controlled how they lived and what they thought.

Things to Do

1. Find and list information in the text above which supports the views expressed in Source B.

2. (a) Why do you think paintings like the one in Source A were often put up in medieval churches?

   (b) What effect do you think they had on people who looked at them?

Scotland in the Middle Ages 400 – 1450 AD

7.2 What was a parish church like?

IN THE MIDDLE Ages most of Scotland was divided up into local areas called parishes. Each parish had its own small church, its priest and its local saint. The parish priest was called the rector. His main job was to perform the mass and to baptise, marry and bury his flock of parishioners.

All families in the parish were supposed to pay a teind, or a tenth of their income, to the Church. The rector's salary came from a share of the teinds. As the local people had little money, he was usually paid in eggs, cheese or grain. He also had a piece of local land called the glebe where he could grow food. In the burghs, a priest could earn some extra money teaching in a school. Despite this, many parish priests were very poorly paid. It was difficult to attract enough able men to this job in the Church.

Many parish churches were simple buildings with little ornament about them. They were rectangular with a rounded apse and a plain stone altar at the eastern end. Many parish churches had earthen floors and roofs of turf divot, but some churches were very splendid. These were often chapels for an important noble family, an abbey or a college. After 1400, as Scotland became a wealthier kingdom, more money was spent on paintings, sculpture and furnishings to turn the churches into beautiful houses of God. The burgh churches in the growing towns, such as St Giles in Edinburgh, were decorated by the rich merchant guilds.

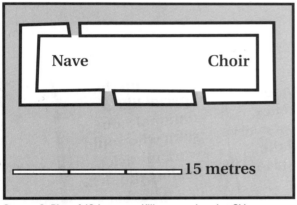

Source A: Plan of 13th century Kilbrannan chapel at Skipness

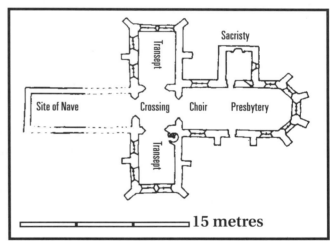

Source B: Plan of 15th century Seton Collegiate Church

Things to Do

1. Why were parish priests poorly paid?

2. Why were some churches much more richly decorated than others?

3. Look at Sources A and B. Find out or work out the meaning of the following terms: nave, choir, transept, presbytery, sacristy.

4. Sources A and B show the ground plan of two medieval Scottish churches. Find and describe as many differences as you can between them. Which of these was the wealthier church? Explain why you think this.

Scotland in the Middle Ages 400 – 1450 AD

7.3 Why was St Andrews Cathedral a wealthy church?

THE FIRST churchmen to live in St Andrews were Culdee monks. These were men of the old Celtic Church who called themselves servants of God (or Celi De in Gaelic). The bones of St Andrew were believed to be held there, so many pilgrims travelled to this small town in Fife to pray at the saint's shrine.

In the 1120s a group of canons or priests founded a church and priory in the town. These canons belonged to the order of St Augustine. In the 1160s their Bishop Arnold began to build a cathedral which was to be the largest church in Scotland. It was over 100 metres in length and built in a style fashionable in much of northern England.

In 1192 the Pope in Rome recognised Scotland as "the special daughter of the Church." The Archbishop of York was no longer the overlord of the Church in Scotland. The leading churchman in Scotland was now the Bishop of St Andrews. He could collect the income from over 235 parishes in central and eastern Scotland. William Fraser of St Andrews was the first churchman to call himself Bishop of the Scots in 1279.

The king and other landowners often gave gifts to the Church. Pilgrims to St Andrews also left offerings at the shrine of this popular saint. Sometimes the dying gave land to the Church in the hope that this good work would help them to get into heaven. Rents from this land were collected very carefully by the canons. Other Christians left sums of money so that daily prayers could be said for their soul after their death. These gifts to the Church made it very wealthy.

Things to Do

1. Why was the Bishop of St Andrews the most important churchman in Scotland?

2. Write down three things which made the cathedral at St Andrews wealthy.

3. Why did many medieval Scots leave money and land to the Church?

4. Look at Source B on page 63. Why do you think there was a wall around the cathedral precinct?

5. Study Source A. Why was St Andrews a successful shrine?
   How would having a successful shrine benefit the ordinary townspeople of St Andrews?

> To attract medieval tourists a town needed relics. But almost every town had the bones of its local saint and pilgrims were increasingly choosy. A successful shrine had to have something special like a national saint, a saint who could work miracles healing the sick, or a relic that was closely connected to the life of Christ.

Source A: From a modern book about medieval relics

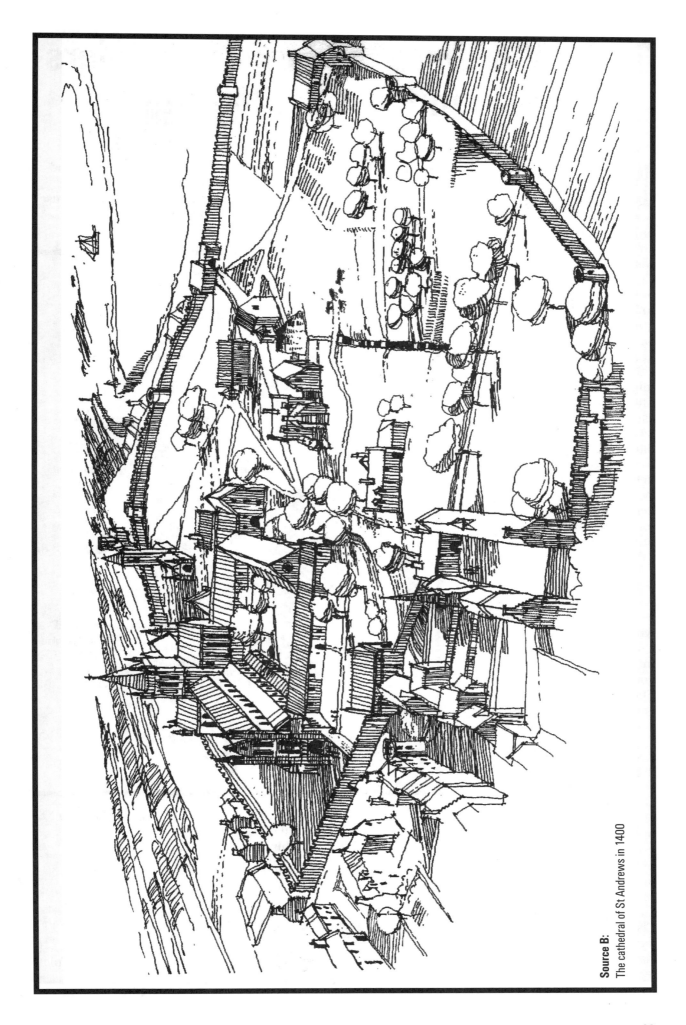

Source B:
The cathedral of St Andrews in 1400

Scotland in the Middle Ages 400 – 1450 AD

7.4 Why were the monastic orders important for Scotland?

MONKS WERE men who devoted their lives to the service of God. They lived together in an order or religious community in an abbey or monastery. There were monks in the old Celtic Church who were often very holy men who lived as hermits. In Norman times, new orders or groups of monks came to Scotland from England and Europe.

Some of these monks followed the Rule of St Benedict. They took vows of obedience, silence and humility. They worshipped seven times each day in the abbey chapel, but they also had to work at tasks decided by their Abbot or Prior. With the help of pious kings like David I, these Benedictines founded abbeys at Kelso, Dunfermline, Paisley and Kilwinning.

The Cistercian Order came to Scotland in the 1100s. They were a French order led by St Bernard. He was a nobleman who gave up his wealth and led a life of piety mixed with hard manual labour. His followers vowed to work and pray hard. The first Cistercian abbeys in Scotland were at Melrose and Newbattle.

The kings of Scotland welcomed the Cistercians to Scotland. To have abbeys was a sign that Scotland was a civilised, Christian land. They were also very profitable. The monks were often granted estates in wild places like the hilly border lands. They drained marshes and cleared the forests, turning wilderness into good farmland. The Melrose Cistercians were expert sheep farmers, while their brothers at Newbattle operated coal and lead mines. The monks brought new farming ideas to Scotland from their abbeys abroad and introduced many new vegetables and fruits. They also helped to develop Scotland's industries such as fishing and textiles. The abbeys became centres of great wealth because of their success in trade.

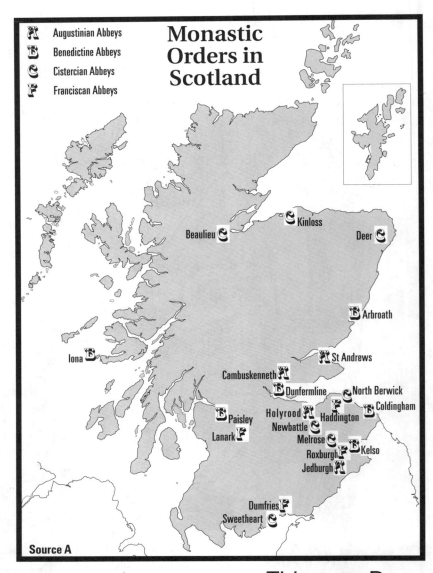

Source A

Things to Do

1. (a) What vows did monks take?
   (b) Why do you think they took these vows?

2. What evidence is there in Source A that the monastic orders prospered in Scotland?

3. What were the main orders in Scotland? Where were most abbeys to be found? What does this tell you about the kingdom of the Scots in the 1200s?

4. Why do you think the monastic orders were so successful in farming, trade and business?

7.5 Why did monasteries and abbeys flourish in Scotland?

JEDBURGH ABBEY was one of the earliest monasteries in Scotland. It was founded by David I and Bishop John of Glasgow in 1138 for a group of Augustinian canons. These churchmen were not secluded monks but were able to leave the abbey to work as priests in the neighbouring parishes.

The kings of Scotland founded monasteries because it was a good Christian thing to do. They also knew that monasteries would become wealthy and would help the kingdom to become more prosperous. Monasteries also provided the educated, learned men that the king needed to help him to run Scotland.

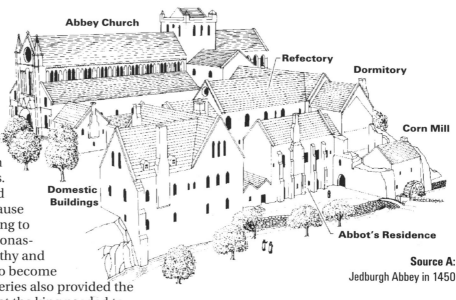

Source A: Jedburgh Abbey in 1450

> I David, by the Grace of God King of Scots, at God's prompting and for the benefit of my soul have founded a monastery in the town of Jedworth in which I have established canons regular. To provide for them I give and confirm by this my charter, the monastery of Jedworth with everything in it, the tithes of the villages of the whole parish namely the towns of Jedworth and Langtoun, and in the village of Crailing one and a half ploughgates of land and three acres together with two dwellings. Also a tenth of the benefit from my royal forest of Teviotdale and all the rents due to the same monastery. Also the right to graze animals near my woodlands and take timber from the woods. Also payment from the people of Jedworth for grinding flour at the abbey mill, and also a saltworks near Stirling.

Source B: The Royal Charter to the monastery at Jedburgh, 1147

Things to Do

1. Why were monasteries useful to the Scottish kingdom?

2. According to Source B, why did King David found an abbey at Jedburgh? How did he make sure that the Jedburgh canons had a good source of income?

3. 'Jedburgh was a flourishing and successful Abbey.' Does Source A support or disprove this statement? Give a reason for your opinion.

Scotland in the Middle Ages 400 – 1450 AD

7.6 Who were the Friars?

THE FIRST FRIARS were religious men who felt that the medieval Church had become too wealthy. They also thought that it was wrong to shut themselves away in a monastery or abbey. Therefore, the friars took a vow to live simply like the early Christians. They gave up their wealth, helped the poor, cared for the sick and preached the word of God. They lived amongst the ordinary people, usually in the main towns.

The friars belonged to separate orders, or groups, which began in Europe. The Franciscans vowed to live in poverty like their Italian founder, St Francis of Assisi. They were called the Greyfriars because they wore a grey habit or robe.

The Dominicans or Blackfriars were known for their learning. They set up schools and spent much of their time teaching about religion. They were invited into Scotland by King Alexander II in 1230. Alexander may have met their founder, St Dominic, while he was a young student in Paris. The Dominicans were later given the job of finding heretics, those who held different religious opinions from the Church. For this reason they were nicknamed 'the hounds of the Lord' which is *Domini canes* in Latin.

The friars were very disciplined, they worked hard and were soon respected. The first Dominican bishop in Britain was Clement of Dunblane in 1233. At first the friars lived by begging in the streets. By 1400 they had been given enough money to build friaries, which were like monasteries but were usually built in the centre of a burgh.

Source A: A friary in medieval Aberdeen

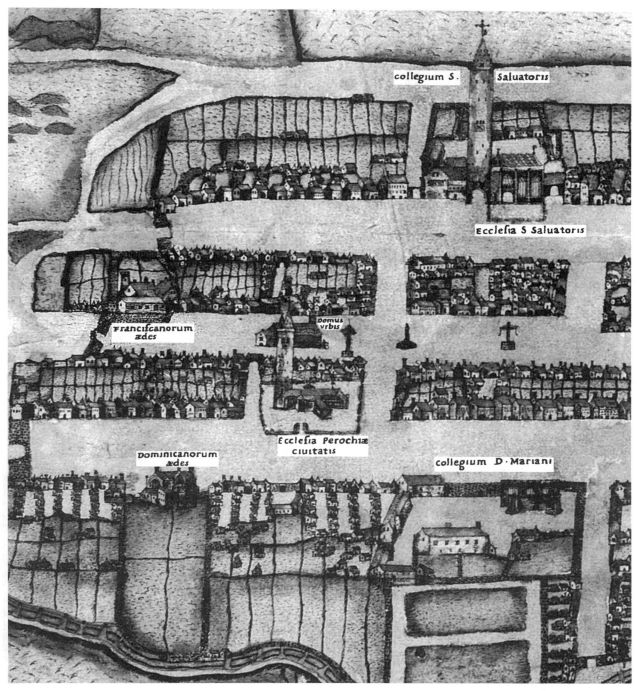

Source B: Evidence of the friars in St Andrews

Things to Do

1. (a) Who were the friars and what did they want to do?
   (b) How were they different from monks?

2. Look at Sources A and B. Find and write in your jotter two things about these sources which tells you that the friar orders were successful.

3. Source B shows St Andrews in the late Middle Ages. What evidence is there that the friars were an important part of medieval daily life in that burgh?

4. Use your school or class library to find out more about the friars. Choose one of the following orders to investigate: Franciscans, Dominicans, Carmelites, Trinitarians.
   Find out what was special about that order and report back to your group.

Scotland in the Middle Ages 400 – 1450 AD

7.7 Why did the Church run the schools in medieval Scotland?

MOST SCHOOLS in medieval Scotland were founded and run by the Church. The Church greatly valued learning. All priests needed to have a general education to carry out their duties, but the Church also needed men with special skills in subjects like theology and law. The only educated men who could act as teachers were churchmen. Poorly paid priests could earn extra money by teaching in a grammar school. Cathedrals needed music in their religious services, so they often ran a 'sang schule'. Talented boys were given a musical, as well as a general, education.

There were grammar schools in many Scottish towns. Aberdeen had a school with a Master of Grammar and Logic as early as 1256. Here boys learned Latin so that they could enter the priesthood. By 1450 Arithmetic, French, Greek and Hebrew were also taught in some Scottish schools. There were monastery schools too. The school at the Cistercian Abbey at Kinloss was set up to educate boys from wild Highland areas.

Sometimes money was left by wealthy benefactors to provide school places for boys from poor families. After 1300, Town Councils helped to pay the cost of education for boys of promise. There were also some schools for girls, known as sewing schools, run by nuns.

> ON entering the school, the boy knelt on the ground to salute Christ and the Virgin Mother of God with a short prayer. Work began at 7 am with an hour of Latin grammar. Those who made mistakes were punished by the master's cane. At 8 am, after punishment, there was a public lecture on one of the Latin writers. After breakfast, there was private study of Latin from 10 am to 11.30, when the boys were allowed into the town. The afternoon was spent on Latin, logic and arithmetic from 2 until 5 pm when there was an hour for disputation or argument. At 6 pm the boys went to chapel to sing prayers to God. The day ended at 7 pm.

Source A: A day in a medieval Grammar School

Source B: Students at a lecture

Things to Do

1. Find at least two reasons why the Church ran the schools in medieval Scotland. Explain each reason you have found.

2. Using Source A draw up a timetable for a pupil at a medieval school.

Time	Subject / Activity
7.00 am	Short prayer then Latin grammar

3. Using Source A and Source B, how many differences can you find between schools then and now? Write these differences down in two columns headed *Medieval Schools* and *Schools Today*.

7.8 Why did many Scots have to study in Europe?

MANY medieval Scots were famous as learned scholars. One of the greatest of all medieval thinkers was born at Duns in Berwickshire. He was known as John Duns Scotus and was a Franciscan friar. After finishing grammar school at Haddington, he studied and taught at the universities of Oxford, Paris and Cologne. He was famed throughout Europe as a Bible scholar and a philosopher.

Another Scot, Michael Scottus, studied at Oxford, Paris and Padua. For many years he lived in the Moorish city of Toledo in southern Spain. He studied Arabic to learn the secrets of medicine and science which Arab scholars had collected. Due to his interest in alchemy and astrology, he became known as 'the Wizard of the North'.

In the 1200s, some Scots went to study at Oxford and Cambridge, but the wars with England put an end to this. Instead, most Scottish scholars followed Duns Scotus to colleges in Europe. The most popular were Paris, Orleans, Cologne and the university at Louvain in Flanders. As a result, Scots lived and travelled throughout Europe. They could see beyond England to the opportunities across the continent.

There were no official colleges in Scotland until 1412 when the first Scottish university was founded in the rich cathedral town of St Andrews. The College of St Salvator was founded, also in St Andrews, in 1450. A College of Arts was begun in Glasgow in 1451. Leading churchmen, merchants and the Scottish kings could all see the benefit which education brought to the country.

Scotland's Older Universities

University	Date
St Andrews University	1412
St Salvators College, St Andrews	1450
Glasgow University	1451
King's College, Aberdeen	1494
St Leonards College, St Andrews	1513
The College of Surgeons	1505
St Marys College, St Andrews	1538
Edinburgh University	1585
Marischal College, Aberdeen	1593
Fraserburgh University	1600

Source A: Foundation dates of Scotland's older universities.

Things to Do

1. (a) What was unusual about the careers of John Duns Scotus and Michael Scottus?
   (b) Why could they not continue their studies in Scotland?
   (c) Do you think this was a good or a bad thing?

2. What does the number of colleges in Source A tell you about the Scottish attitude to learning?

3. (a) What are the main buildings in the view of medieval Old Aberdeen shown on page 70?
   (b) How do they compare with the other buildings in this town?
   (c) What does that tell you about the importance of the Church in the Middle Ages?

Source B: King's College in Old Aberdeen

Unit 8

Burgh Life

8.1	What did a burgh look like?	72
8.2	Why were burghs founded?	73
8.3	Who were the burgesses?	75
8.4	Why were Guilds important?	76
8.5	Who were the burgh craftsmen?	77
8.6	When were fairs held?	78
8.7	How big were Scotland's burghs?	79
8.8	What were Scotland's links with Europe?	81

8.1 What did a burgh look like?

A BURGH WAS a small town. At first, the houses were made of wooden posts with mud and wattle walls and thatched roofs. The streets were just earth that had been trodden down by feet and carts. Later, by the 1300s, some stone houses with tiled roofs were built in the bigger, richer burghs. Some streets were cobbled and had ditches to take away the rain and refuse.

Most burghs were surrounded by a strong wooden stockade and a deep ditch. Often the burgh was near to a castle or similar stronghold. At either end of the burgh, there were strong wooden ports or gates which were closed at night to keep the burgh folk secure. During the day, porters or gate-keepers collected tolls from people bringing goods into the burgh to sell. Outside the stockade was the burgh muir—rough pasture land where the burgh folk could graze cattle or sheep.

Often there was just one main gate or High Street from which ran smaller lanes, wynds or closes. At the back of most houses there was a long narrow strip of land. This was called a 'toft'. This was fenced off so that each family could keep chickens or a pig there. The burgh folk also grew vegetables like kale and peas on their tofts.

There was usually one large open space. This was the market place, marked with a cross and often containing the burgh weighing scales or Tron. Later burghs had a Tolbooth nearby. This was a stone tower where the burgh council kept its valuables. The biggest building in the burgh was the Town Kirk. As the burgh grew richer, other churches were built. Some burghs also used their wealth to replace their stockade and build stronger stone walls.

Source A: Plan of Medieval Glasgow

> THE whole of the people of the burgh of Inverness have come to an agreement with me that when I have made an earthen dyke around the burgh, they will enclose it with a sound palisade, erected on that dyke, and when the burgh has been thus enclosed, they will maintain the palisade and keep it in good and sound repair.

Source B: From the charter of King William to the Burgh of Inverness

Things to Do

1. Why would the burgh folk be keen to build defences as described in Source B? What benefits do you think the king would get from helping to protect the burgh?

2. If you live in or near an old burgh, investigate its early history. Find out when it was founded, how it was defended, where the original gates and ports were. Look for evidence of its medieval origins such as street names, a market cross or the old Town Kirk. Try to draw a rough plan or map of the burgh in medieval times. Compare the burgh you are investigating with the one shown in Source A.

Scotland in the Middle Ages 400 – 1450 AD

8.2 Why were burghs founded?

THROUGHOUT the Middle Ages, much of the Scottish countryside was a lawless and dangerous place. It was difficult for merchants to move their goods around a country which had many thieves and bandits. A burgh was a safe place where trade could be protected and controlled. For a long time, burghs were the only places where you were legally allowed to buy and sell certain goods.

A burgh was also a fair place to trade as the quality of goods sold there was checked. Each burgh had a set of official weights and scales to make sure that no one was cheated when they bought something. Prices in the marketplace were fixed by burgh law. After 1200 the king allowed coins to be minted in many burghs. These were silver pennies, halfpennies and even farthings, or quarter-pennies, coins needed for the burghs' growing trade on market days.

Royal Burghs were a source of wealth for the king. Every householder had to pay an annual rent to the king's sheriff. Newcomers had to pay a fee if they wanted to settle inside the stockade. All goods sold in the market were taxed. The king could also collect customs duties from ports like Berwick and Aberdeen.

Things to Do

1. *Burgh merchants had a monopoly of trade in their area.*

   Use the information on this page, and a dictionary, to explain the meaning of this sentence.

   Do you think it is true?

2. Why do you think the kings of Scotland were very keen to establish burghs and did a lot to help them to grow?

3. Look at Source B carefully. Why do you think Edinburgh was a good place to found a burgh?

> WITHIN the Sheriffdom of Lanark, no one may buy wool or leather hides, or any other merchandise, or make broad cloth, except the merchants of the burgh of Lanark. If any stranger merchant shall come into this Sheriffdom buying wool, hides or similar merchandise, he shall be seized and detained with his goods.

Source A: The rights of the burgh of Lanark, 1285 by King Alexander III

Scotland in the Middle Ages 400 – 1450 AD

EDINBURGH

Source A: **The burgh of Edinburgh in 1100 AD** In 1100 AD Edinburgh was a very small settlement. There were, perhaps, thirty or forty dwellings clustered around the fort on the rock. It was a well-defended site but far too close to the southern border to be the capital of the kingdom. However if the king and his followers were garrisoned in the fort during the winter, life in the burgh could be lively enough.

Scotland in the Middle Ages 400 – 1450 AD

8.3 Who were the burgesses?

THE BURGESSES were wealthy merchants who lived in the burghs. They were freemen who had special rights or liberties. These liberties were protected by the king and were recorded on a special document called the Burgh Charter. The Charter was so valuable that it was usually kept in a metal strongbox in the Tolbooth under lock and key.

Burgesses enjoyed special trading rights. They were the only people allowed to deal in valuable commodities such as furs and hides. They could send goods around the kingdom without paying tolls. Only burgesses were allowed to trade with foreign merchants and buy luxuries like beeswax or wine. Sometimes they also had privileges which allowed them to control hunting and fishing in the marshes and on the coasts near their town.

As burgesses were the only people who could vote or be elected to the Burgh Council, only burgesses could become the Burgh Provost or town leader. The Baillies, judges who sat on the Burgh Court and sentenced petty criminals, had to be burgesses. Burgesses enjoyed a lot of rights and privileges which ordinary people did not have.

In return for these rights, burgesses had to take an oath of loyalty to the Burgh Council and the king. In the early days of the burghs, around 1150, they had to keep a set of weapons in the house and be ready to defend the town. After 1200 they paid an annual burgess fee to the king instead. In wartime, they had to be ready to lend or give money to the king to pay for his troops.

Source A: A burgess's house from the late Middle Ages.

ROBERT, by the grace of God King of Scots, greetings to all good men of his land. Know ye that we have granted to the burgesses of our burgh of Aberdeen, their heirs and successors... mills, waters, fishings, petty customs, tolls, courts, weights, measures and all other privileges. We also grant that the said burgesses may perform every kind of tillage, erect dwelling houses and other buildings, dig fuel, as they shall think best to do. The said burgesses will pay to us and our heirs, two hundred and thirteen pounds, six shillings and eightpence sterling into our chamber.

Source B: The liberties of Aberdeen's burgesses, 1319.

Things to Do

1. Rewrite Source B in your own words, explaining the privileges which King Robert granted to the burgesses of Aberdeen. Use a dictionary to work out the meanings of any words you do not know.

2. Try and work out how the burgesses could make money from each of the privileges mentioned in the charter. Be able to explain why the king granted these rights to the burgh merchants.

3. Look carefully at the burgess's house in Source A. What tells you that such houses were built by wealthy families?

8.4 Why were Guilds important?

IN SCOTLAND'S biggest towns, most burgesses were also members of the Merchants' Guild, which controlled all the trade in the burgh. It made sure that only local burgesses traded in valuable commodities like furs and wool. Foreign merchants in the burgh were watched by the Guild to make sure that they did not make illegal deals. It sold licences to countryside hawkers, pedlars or packmen which allowed them to come into the burgh on market day to sell their wares. The quality of food and drink that was on sale in the burgh was checked by the Guild.

Members of the Guild swore an oath to help their fellow guildsmen in times of trouble. In some burghs, guildsmen called each other 'brother'. If a member cheated another guildsman, the guild could fine him. They promised to help members who fell on hard times, and to support their widows and orphans. Guildsmen who fought or quarrelled with each other were fined very heavily.

By 1450 the Guild members had taken over all the official jobs in the burgh. The Scottish Parliament passed a law in 1469 which gave the guildsmen great power. From that year onwards the guildsmen simply elected themselves to the Burgh Council. They used this power to keep down the craftsmen of the burgh. Craftsmen could not join a Guild unless they gave up making things with their hands.

> **WE ORDER** that all tenants and peasants bringing foodstuffs into the burgh shall bring them to the guildhouse, for their fitness for sale and their price to be established. Those selling rotten foodstuffs shall be fined. We also order that no one dare to place filth or any dust or ashes on the common street, in the marketplace, or on the banks of the Tweed, to the hurt of passers-by. Anyone who does this shall be fined eight shillings.

Source A: From the guild laws of Berwick, 1430

Source B: Scenes from a medieval market, 1400

Things to Do

1. How did Guilds control burgh trade? Why do you think they did this?
2. Why do you think guildsmen promised to help each other in times of trouble?
3. (a) According to Source A, what kinds of daily problems did the Guild try to solve?
   (b) How did they punish offenders?
4. How do you think the Guilds actually controlled the sale of goods in markets like that shown in Source B?

Scotland in the Middle Ages 400 – 1450 AD

8.5 Who were the burgh craftsmen?

BURGESSES AND GUILDSMEN were traders and merchants, but craftsmen made the products that were sold at the market stalls. Most craftsmen worked in their own homes. Sometimes they had a workshop on the ground floor and lived above it.

Nearly all craftsmen carried out only one stage in making something. Cloth was made by men like the fullers, spinners, websters and dyers. Leather goods were made by skinners, tanners, soutters, and saddlers. The craftsmen involved in making food such as butchers, millers and bakers were strictly controlled by the Burgh Council.

In the early Middle Ages, there were few skilled craftsmen in Scotland. Wealthy people imported luxury goods from France, England and the Low Countries. Only poor folk bought things made by local craftsmen. After 1400 the quality of Scottish made goods improved, partly because foreign craftsmen from Europe had come to Scotland and passed on their skills.

The craftsman was helped by his journeyman and apprentice. These were younger men or boys who were learning the job and might some day create a 'master's piece' to show their skill. If they could convince the other craftsmen that they were worthy, and that they were sober and serious, they were allowed to join the 'craft'. Each craft had a Deacon whose job was to test the journeymen and make sure that the quality of craftsmanship was kept high.

In some burghs, particular craftsmen settled in the same part of town. So some old streets or lanes have a name that tells you who used to work there, such as Candlemaker Row in Edinburgh.

Source A: Articles made by craftsmen in Scotland c 1400

After 1400 it is clear that economic conditions favoured craftsmen at home. More weapons, artillery and armour were manufactured in Scotland than were imported from Europe. There was also a great deal of building work on churches and castles.

Source B: From a modern history book

Things to Do

1. What are the objects shown in Source A? What are they made of? Why do you think they have survived until modern times?

2. According to the writer of Source B, which crafts prospered after 1400? What kinds of workers would have done well at this time?

3. How did you get to join a craft? What did you have to prove?

4. List the crafts mentioned in the text. Use a good dictionary to find out what these men did.

5. If you live in or near an old burgh, look at the street names in the oldest part of town. Try to work out how these streets got their names. What kind of people used to live and work on that street?

Scotland in the Middle Ages 400 – 1450 AD

8.6 When were fairs held?

FAIRS COULD only be held at the times allowed by the king. A burgh had to ask, or buy, the king's permission which was usually granted by charter. King William the Lion (1165–1214) gave the burgh of Glasgow the right to hold a fair for eight days after 6 July. Aberdeen's fair was granted by King Alexander in 1273. It was to last for two weeks from the feast of the Holy Trinity.

Fairs were the most exciting time in the life of the burgh folk. Stalls, tents and booths sprang up, sometimes outside the burgh on the muir. The king and his court might arrive to watch over the fun. The town was packed with pedlars, hawkers and chapmen selling their wares. The rich merchants used the fair to meet and plan their business for the year ahead. The marketplace was also full of travelling entertainers who went from town to town following the calendar of fairs. Country folk came in to see the acrobats, jugglers, wrestlers, balladeers, musicians and performing beasts. At the Mercat Cross, friars would preach open-air sermons to the crowds, urging them to turn away from these frivolities and look instead to God.

Life during the fair was different. Firstly, the normal burgh trading rules were suspended. Anyone, not just burgesses, could buy the luxuries, such as spices, herbs, wines and fine cloth which were on sale from foreign merchants. Also, the curfew, the law which ordered people to stay in their houses after dark, did not run during the fair. Thirdly, troublemakers such as drunks or hooligans were punished more lightly during 'the fair's peace'. Instead of being tried by the strict Burgh Court, they were brought before a temporary 'Piepowder' or Pedlar's Court.

> THE Prior of Coldingham Priory asks the King and his Council to grant the right to hold a fair at Coldingham on St Cuthbert's Day for fifteen days or for eight in honour of God and St Cuthbert.

Source A: Letter requesting permission to hold a fair

Source B: Medieval entertainers

Things to Do

1. How did burghs gain the right to hold a fair?

2. In what ways was burgh life different during a fair?

3. Why do you think the writer of Source A wanted to hold a fair? What did he hope to gain from it? How do you think the king decided who should be allowed to hold a fair?

4. Use the information on this page to write a short description of your visit to a burgh fair. Describe what you saw, heard and smelt. Describe what you bought and how you spent your time there.

5. Find out more about old fairs in your area. Where were they held? When were they held? How do we know that they existed? What do we know about them?

Scotland in the Middle Ages 400 – 1450 AD

8.7 How big were Scotland's burghs?

Source A: The burgh of Dundee in the 1600s

IN 1300 THERE were fifty six burghs in Scotland but none of them was very large by modern standards. Far and away the biggest was Berwick on Tweed, which was a seaport and a secure walled city with about two thousand inhabitants. This was a rich town because it was the centre of the wool trade between Scotland and Europe. Berwick's burgesses paid an annual fee of £333 to the Scottish king and the port raised over £2000 in customs duties.

The other important burghs, Edinburgh, Aberdeen, Stirling and Perth, were much smaller than Berwick. One French chronicler in 1350 said that Edinburgh had about 400 houses in all. Perth was often the capital of Scotland in the Middle Ages, but in 1291 it had only about 100 merchants, craftsmen and householders.

Some burghs, such as Fyvie, Cromarty and Airth, were never very large because there was not enough trade in their area for them to prosper. Other burghs like Crail and Culross were very important places in medieval Scotland but shrunk in size afterwards.

One major burgh simply disappeared. This was Kincardine in the Mearns. Many of Scotland's kings stayed at the massive castle there to hunt in the nearby forests. A large burgh grew up around the fortress. The king's Court was often sited at Kincardine, making it the unofficial capital of Scotland. Today nothing remains of the burgh or the castle.

Things to Do

1. According to the information on this page, what made a burgh important?

2. Why do you think some burghs never grew in size? Suggest some reasons for this.

3. Look at Source A. Although it was drawn in the 1600s, it gives a good idea of what a medieval burgh looked like. What are the main buildings? How was Dundee defended? Why was it a good site for a burgh?

4. Study Source B on page 80 and compare it with Source B in Unit 8.2. How did this area change during the Middle Ages? Find and list as many changes as you can. Give an explanation of why you think these changes took place.

5. With a partner, discuss the mystery of Kincardine. Write down all the things that could have happened to make this burgh vanish completely. Choose the most likely reason and be ready to explain why you chose it.

Scotland in the Middle Ages 400 – 1450 AD

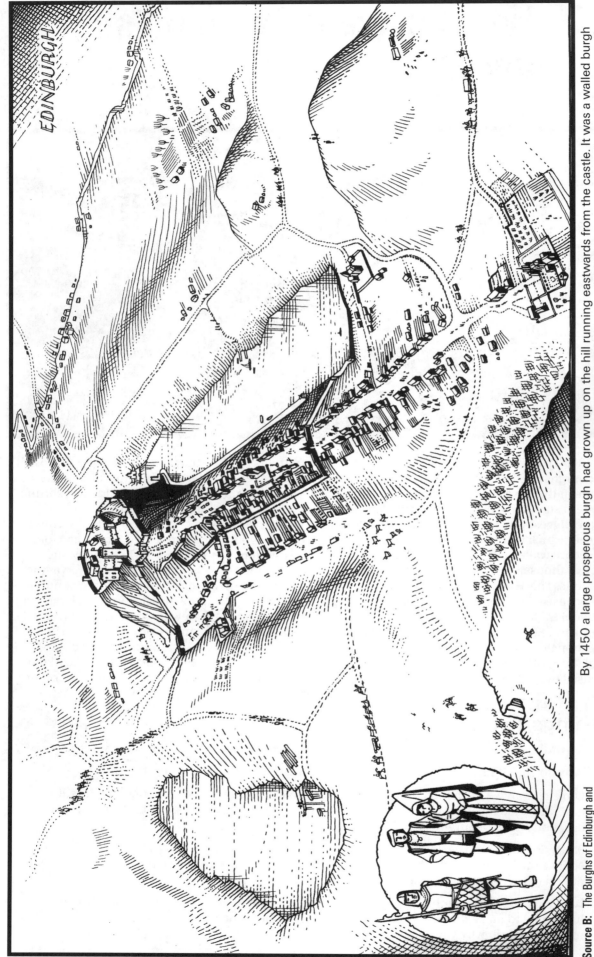

Source B: The Burghs of Edinburgh and Canongate in 1450 AD

By 1450 a large prosperous burgh had grown up on the hill running eastwards from the castle. It was a walled burgh with an open marketplace below the castle gate. Many of the burgesses had orchards and gardens behind their houses on the long High Street. Outside the town wall was the separate burgh of Canongate centred on the Abbey of Holyrood.

Scotland in the Middle Ages 400 – 1450 AD

8.8 What were Scotland's links with Europe?

IN THE MIDDLE Ages, travel by sea was often faster and safer than travel overland. Scotland was separated from England by the wild and hilly Border country and by the moors of Cumbria and Northumberland. As there were no proper roads leading south, England was a strange and distant country.

Most of Scotland's trade was with Europe. By 1280 Berwick had large colonies of Flemish and German merchants who lived and worked in their separate Red and White Halls. They bought wool from the Border abbeys and baronial estates. The wool was then shipped to the Low Countries, to cloth towns like Bruges, Courtrai and Ghent. There it was worked into a finer cloth than the Scots could make. The Flemish merchants also bought skins and salted fish, mostly salmon and herring.

After 1400 there were many Scottish merchants across Europe. There were streets and alleyways named after Scottish merchants in cities as far apart as Danzig, Stockholm, Bergen, Bruges, Rouen and Bordeaux. However, most Scots traded in the Low Countries. For many years the city of Middelburg and the town of Veere in the modern Netherlands were the Scots 'staple'. This means that they were the ports which had the rights to control trade with Scotland. The records from these towns tell us what the Scots bought from Europe in exchange for their wool and leather.

Sent to Customers in Scotland

34 ells of velvet	£17	5s	0d
2 pieces of thick twilled cotton cloth	£1	4s	0d
3 pieces of chequered cloth	£2	11s	0d
50 lbs of almonds	£12	6s	0d
50 lbs of rice		7s	0d
17 lbs of pepper		19s	0d
1 roll of canvas		7s	0d
a little tin of ginger		7s	6d
half a ream of paper		1s	6d
2 vestments or robes for priests	£2	7s	0d
3 puncheons or wooden casks of wine	£7	17s	0d
2 barrels of apples		11s	6d
2 lbs of saffron dye	£1	0s	0d
25 cases of sugar	£8	2s	0d
drugs	£10	8s	0d
125 ells of linen cloth	£3	2s	6d
4 feather beds	£4	0s	0d
12 pillows	£1	4s	0d
12 candlesticks		13s	4d
3 dozen pewter dishes	£9	14s	9d
1 dozen table napkins		9s	0d
1 barrel gunpowder	£4	16s	4d
2 silver chalices	£13	0s	5d
2 black bonnets		6s	0d

Source A: Ledger of Andrew Haliburton, merchant at Middelburg 1492 – 1503

Things to Do

1. Use an atlas to find the European cities mentioned in the text. Mark them on a blank map of Europe, then link them with coloured lines to show Scotland's trade routes in the Middle Ages. Give your map a suitable heading.

2. (a) Why do you think so much cloth was brought into Scotland from abroad?
   (b) What kinds of people do you think ordered these goods from Haliburton?
   (c) Look at Source A. What does the ledger tell you about the state of industry inside Scotland?
   (d) What were the largest items imported to Scotland? Which were the most expensive?

Unit 9

Country Life

9.1	Why was farming difficult in medieval Scotland?	83
9.2	What was a toun?	84
9.3	How was the land farmed?	85
9.4	What tools were used on medieval farms?	87
9.5	Who were the neyfs?	88
9.6	What did the Scots eat?	89
9.7	What were Scottish houses like?	90
9.8	Why was wool so important to medieval Scotland?	91

9.1 Why was farming difficult in medieval Scotland?

COMPARED to France, the Low Countries or England, Scotland was a poor country with a small population. It was not an easy country to farm in. The Scots found it difficult to grow enough food for themselves and never had a great surplus for trading overseas. Famine was a real hazard of life in medieval Scotland.

🌾 Large parts of Scotland were mountainous and too wild for any kind of farming. Much of the land was covered in deep forest or wilderness. There was very little arable land—far less than a tenth of the kingdom. A large amount of the soil was sour and stony.

🌾 The summer was very short and the climate was cold and wet. Many crops were difficult to grow in Scotland. Wheat would only grow in a few sheltered, warmer places like the Moray coast, East Lothian and the Mearns.

🌾 There was rich soil in the wide river valleys but these were undrained and marshy. Farmers could not use this good soil in case it flooded and turned to bog. They had to grow their crops on higher land which was dry but poor in minerals.

🌾 There were no proper roads, just a few beaten tracks across the hills used by merchants and pedlars. Country villages were cut off from each other. This meant that even if a farmer had extra food, it was not easy to exchange or sell it at a market.

🌾 Disease was common amongst the livestock. A farmer's hard-won wealth could be wiped out by bad weather and bad luck.

> THE country is difficult and hard to travel. To a man on horseback, the hills are impassable, save here and there. The woods are full of stags and roe deer and other woodland beasts. But in the upland districts, and along the highlands, the fields are less productive, except only in oats and barley. The country is very hideous, interspersed with moors and marshy fields, muddy and dirty.

Source A: A 15th century description of Scotland's countryside

> IN the year 1310, so great was the famine and dearth of provisions in the kingdom of Scotland, that in most places many folk were driven, by the pinch of hunger, to feed on the flesh of horses and other unclean cattle. In the year 1344 there was so great a pestilence among the fowls, that men utterly shrank from eating, or even looking upon, chickens as though they were unclean and smitten with leprosy; and so nearly the whole of that species was destroyed.

Source B: From a 15th century Scottish chronicle

Things to Do

Scotland was a difficult land to farm. Make a list of the reasons for this which are given on this page.

Scotland in the Middle Ages 400 – 1450 AD

9.2 What was a toun?

A TOUN WAS the Scots name for a small farming village or township. Most touns had from two to six houses with a family in each house. Almost all Scots in the Middle Ages lived in touns and worked on the land as peasant farmers.

In each toun, there might be one or two main tenant farmers who were responsible for making sure that the land was farmed properly and that the rent was paid to the laird. These men were called husbandmen, and sometimes a farm area was called a husbandland. There were other families of neyfs or cottars who worked on a small share of the husbandland.

All touns had a feudal lord and belonged to an estate. The lord could be a baron in a nearby castle or hall, or perhaps the king or his sheriff, or he could even be the abbot of an abbey or monastery. The husbandman paid his rent to the lord in money or in kind, which meant he had to hand over goods such as meal, grain or butter. Many of Scotland's wealthiest estates belonged to abbeys like Kelso in the Borders. This was because the monks encouraged their tenant farmers to work hard and try new, better ways of farming.

In the richer lowlands, touns were often so close together that the boundaries between them had to be marked out carefully with stones. In the Highlands touns, called *bailtean* in Gaelic, were often miles apart and isolated by moorland, hills and bog.

> The touns were mostly successful farming units which generated enough food to feed Scotland's population well nine years out of ten. The husbandmen perfected a system of farming that was well suited to Scotland's climate and geography.

Source A: From a modern history book

> Most touns were isolated, their inhabitants were ignorant and superstitious subsistence farmers who scratched a living from the soil by carrying out the age-old farming customs which they had learned from their fathers. Families struggled to feed themselves, and years of effort and thrift could be lost in one bad harvest. These were people completely at the mercy of the climate.

Source B: From a modern history book

Things to Do

1. What was a husbandman and what did he do?

2. Why did the farmers in the touns have to pay rent to the laird? How did they pay that rent?

3. The writers of Sources A and B disagree about the success of the touns. In what ways are their opinions different? Why do you think they have such different views?

9.3 How was the land farmed?

MOST TOUNS had only a little arable land for growing crops. The good land was called infield because it was close to the houses. Sometimes it was called muckkitland because the people spread their own dung and animal manure on it as fertiliser. The land further away from the toun was called outfield. It was rough, stony land which was only used as pasture for grazing beasts.

There were no square fields like those we have today. Instead, the good land was divided up into long ploughed strips. Along these strips the soil was piled up into mounds called runrigs. The husbandmen grew their crops along the top of these rigs. Between the rigs were ditches called baulks that filled with water and weeds.

On some estates, no one had the same rigs two years in a row. Each spring the husbandmen in the toun gathered at the kirk to draw their new rigs in a lottery. That was done to share out the good land in a fair way, but it meant that no one worked hard at improving their soil for they might lose it the following year.

The soil was often poor. There were few cattle, so good dung was scarce. Farmers would plant crops on a rig for four or five years, then it would be left alone for two years. This rest or fallow period gave the land a chance to recover.

As well as paying rent to work the land, most husbandmen and neyfs had to perform services for their lord. This meant they had to work on his rigs for a certain number of days in the year, as well as on their own.

> THE corn is very good but they do not produce as much of it as they might because they do not cultivate the soil properly. They plough the land only once, then they sow the corn seed and cover it by means of a harrow or wooden rake. Nothing more is done until they cut the corn.

Source A: From a 15th century Spanish traveller's description of Scotland

> THE common people of Scotland have no permanent holdings of land but instead hire or lease strips of land for four or five years at the pleasure of the lord of the soil. Because of this they do not bother to build good houses or work hard at the land, nor do they plant trees or hedges to protect their crops, nor do they waste their valuable dung on the land.

Source B: From a 16th century English writer's description of Scotland

Things to Do

1. Why did medieval farmers not bother to improve the land they worked on?

2. What was wrong with the Scottish way of farming according to the writers of Sources A and B?

3. Look for the rigs and baulks in Source C on page 86. Why do you think there was so much infield near this toun?

   How is it different from modern fields?

   What is missing?

Scotland in the Middle Ages 400 – 1450 AD

Source C: Rigs outside Arbroath in the 1600s

9.4 What tools were used on medieval farms?

FARMERS IN medieval Scotland had very primitive tools. Everything on the farm had to be done by hand as there were no machines.

The main tool was the plough which was used to break up the rough ground after winter so that seeds could be planted in the spring. The old Scots plough was a very heavy and cumbersome object. It was basically a length of heavy wood with a sharp metal coulter on the nose which cut into the soil. Teams of eight oxen and up to four men were needed to keep it moving and steady. Ploughing an acre of land could take more than two days of hard effort.

In very hilly districts where the soil was stony and thin, this heavy plough was no use. Here farmers had to delve or dig using a cas-chrom or crooked spade. After ploughing, the farmers walked along their rigs spreading corn seed by hand. Seeds were then pressed into the earth and covered with soil using a harrow.

At harvest time, the crops were cut with a hand sickle, so everyone was needed to help. The corn was dried by setting it in stooks, then threshed with flails. This was the hard task of separating the grain from the chaff. Many estates had wind or river mills to grind the grain but these belonged to the local lord. He charged a high fee for the use of his mill and the skill of his miller. Many families had a small hand-mill or quern in their houses but this was a slow, tiring way to get flour from grain.

There was never much grain so there was none to spare on feeding beasts during the long winter months. Most cattle were slaughtered in November at Martinmas and their meat was stored in barrels of salt or brine. Farmers, therefore, had to have the skills and tools of butchering and coopering (making barrels).

A MAN who has more than 4 cattle shall rent land from his lord and shall plough and sow to feed his family. A man who has less than 5 cattle, and cannot plough with oxen, must with his hands and feet delve the earth. If any lord will not allow this in his lands, he shall pay a fine of 8 cattle to the king.

Source A: Royal law ordering farmers to plough more of their land, 1214

THE assets of the farm of Alexander Hume of Dunglass were:
- 2,618 sheep
- 248 cattle
- numerous pigs
- chickens
- goats
- 20 bushels of wheat
- 45 bushels of oats and
- 25 bushels of barley.

Source B: A typical farm in the Lothians, 1424

Source C: Harvesting by sickle

Things to Do

1. Why could no one farm on their own in the Middle Ages? What would be the good and bad points of getting others to help you to farm your rigs?
2. Why do you think the Scots used such a heavy, slow plough?
3. Why was there never enough grain to feed cattle?
4. Read Source A. Why do you think several Scottish kings had to order country folk to plough more land than they wanted to?
5. According to Source B, what kinds of farming were done on this typical Lothians farm?

Scotland in the Middle Ages 400 – 1450 AD

9.5 Who were the neyfs?

NEYFS OR SERFS were peasants with very few rights. A large part of the Scottish population in medieval times were neyfs. They were often owned by a baron and were attached to a farm on his estate. If the baron sold or gifted that land to someone, the neyfs were part of the sale. In old documents, they were called *nativi* which means people who are born to the land.

Almost all neyfs were given small pieces of land to work to feed themselves, but much of their time was spent working on the demesnes. The demesnes, or main farm, was made up of the lord's own fields where cereals were grown. The neyf had to perform tasks like ploughing, sowing, tilling, weeding and reaping for his lord without being paid. We know that some neyfs hated their way of life. A letter of 1364 mentions three runaways in Morayshire who had been recaptured and returned to their lord.

By 1400 the word neyf had disappeared from use. Many bought their freedom from their lords. Perhaps so many neyfs died in the plague epidemics that lords had to pay labourers to work their land instead. Now they were cottars who had a hut of their own, a kaleyard around it to grow vegetables and a few acres of poor runrig or arable land. Nevertheless, they still had to pay rent and do services for their lord. They also had to pay high fees to get their corn ground at the lord's mill.

Source A: Order by King David I for the return of runaways, 1125

I COMMAND that the runaways be speedily restored to the church of the Holy Trinity of Dunfermline... and all the runaways from the time of King Edgar until now, wherever they be found.

Source B: Neyfs at work

Things to Do

1. 'Neyfs were slaves.' Find at least three pieces of information in the text above which support this point of view.

2. 'Nefys lived a very hard life.' What evidence of this can you find above?

3. 'The system of neyfs died out by 1400.' Read the text above carefully, then explain in your own words why this happened.

4. 'Neyfs were no better off once they were free.' What information is there in the text for and against this point of view?

Scotland in the Middle Ages 400 – 1450 AD

9.6 What did the Scots eat?

IN YEARS OF FAMINE, when the summer was very wet, the Scots ate very little. However, most years there was enough to go round, even if the diet was basic by modern standards. Most families had two meals a day in good years. They ate food which they had produced and prepared themselves.

There was little wheat grown in Scotland, so bread was expensive and not eaten much by poor people. It was a delicacy for well-off town folk. The main cereals were oats and bere, a rough kind of barley which grows well in cold, wet climates. Poor people, therefore, ate a lot of oatmeal, porridge, oat cakes, bannocks, barley-broth and barley-cake.

Beef was uncommon. It was usually stringy and tasted of the salt brine used to keep it from rotting. As most farms kept sheep for their wool, mutton was an occasional treat. There was usually cheese and milk. In coastal areas, fish and molluscs were available. Inland, people ate salted fish brought to the markets by pedlars. People who lived near highland areas could hunt for rabbit, gamebirds and perhaps a deer. Most families grew their own vegetables, such as peas, green beans and kale, a kind of cabbage. In many touns there were hives to collect honey, the only way of sweetening food. Adults and children alike drank ale or weak beer made from barley.

> THE common people of Scotland stuff themselves with large amounts of mutton and fish, and look on bread as a delicacy or dainty.

Source A: A comment by an Italian traveller, Aeneas Piccolomini, 1435

> Stuff themselves must be an exaggeration, but Aeneas Piccolomini was clearly struck by the amount of animal products eaten and by the absence of wheaten bread. Since white bread was then the most fashionable food, he was probably turning up his nose. Nevertheless a diet based on oatmeal, with animal and fish protein and vitamin C from kale is actually very healthy—probably much healthier than that of most European peasants at this time.

Source B: From a modern history book

Things to Do

1. (a) In what ways is the medieval Scottish diet different from the food you eat today?
   (b) What words could you use to describe it?
   (c) Which foods are the same as those we eat today?
   (d) Which modern foods are missing?
   (e) Why are the two diets so different?

2. Read Source A. Did the writer think the Scots had a good diet or not? Explain your answer.

3. Now read Source B. How does the modern historian who wrote Source B interpret Piccolomini's comments? What does the historian think about the medieval Scottish diet? Do you agree with his opinion?

Scotland in the Middle Ages 400 – 1450 AD

9.7 What were Scottish houses like?

MOST COUNTRY folk in medieval Scotland lived in simple houses made of materials which could be found easily. These houses were usually oblong, about eight metres long and three metres wide. They had a wooden frame with walls of mud and wattle or turf. Roofs were made with turf, heather and thatch. Animal skins were used to cover doors and windows.

A more prosperous family might build a house with stone walls, but this was unusual in lowland Scotland. In the Highlands there was little timber but a lot of stone, and so the folk built 'black houses'. These had inner and outer stone walls with a filling of pressed earth to help keep out the cold wind.

In the winter, cattle and sheep were herded into the house to shelter from the weather. They were roped off from the family's area. The cooking was done on an open fire in a circle of stones in the middle of the flattened earth floor. Food was cooked in a large metal pot or cauldron which hung by chains from the rafters. The main fuel was peat turf. The smoke had to find its own way to the small hole cut in the thatched roof.

There was little furniture in most homes. Box beds were simple wooden frames filled with straw, heather and bracken. Many families had a kist, a wooden chest in which blankets and linens were stored. The main kitchen utensil was a quern, which was a heavy stone used for grinding corn into meal. There would be a water-bucket and perhaps a milk-pail. Meals were eaten from wooden bowls using spoons made of horn or bone.

> THE roofs of the houses in the country are made of turf and the doors of the humbler dwellings are simply made from the skins of oxen.

Source A: From a description of Scotland in 1435 by an Italian visitor

> THE country people made light of the destruction of their homes by the English, saying that with six or eight wooden stakes they would soon have new houses.

Source B: After an English attack on Lothian in 1385

Source C: A black house in the Hebrides

Things to Do

1. Measure out a space eight by three metres in your classroom. Plan out where the box beds and the cooking fire would be placed. How much room does that leave? Why would the people in these houses not worry about lack of space?
   What were the good and bad points of having your animals in the house during winter?

2. Why was it a good idea not to have a stone house, according to Source B?

3. No wooden medieval houses have survived to modern times. How, therefore, do we know what they looked like?

Scotland in the Middle Ages 400 – 1450 AD

9.8 Why was wool so important to medieval Scotland?

WOOL WAS the most important thing that medieval Scotland produced. People needed it to keep themselves warm. They knew how to make linen cloth from flax and leather was used for jackets, belts and footwear. However, a rough grey-brown woollen cloth was the main material used for everyday clothes such as tunics, dresses, stockings and cowls.

Wool was valuable and could be sold to foreign merchants. Wool was Scotland's biggest export. Scotland had a lot of hilly pasture land which was suited to sheep farming. Many noble families herded vast flocks of sheep on their estates. Abbeys like the Cistercian order at Melrose reared thousands of sheep in the Border hills and used their contacts to sell the wool in towns across Europe.

By 1200 Berwick and Perth were rich towns because they exported wool abroad. In the 1370s over 2,000,000 fleeces and 100,000 sheepskins were sent to Europe. In one year alone, 1372, over 9,250 sacks of wool worth more than £40,000 were packed on ships bound for the cities of Northern Europe. This was a small fortune in which the merchants, the king and the ordinary Scot could share.

> NOW by this charter that I, Richard of Moreville, give to God and the church of St Mary of Melrose and to the monks living there, the place in Witelei at the edge of the forest, to make a sheepfold and a house in which the monks can make a fire for the brethren and their herds, and also a house in which they may place their hay.

Source A: A gift to the monks of Melrose Abbey, 1190

> International trade made many of the burgesses in Scotland's towns rich. But what did the trade do for the rest of the Scottish people? When peasants sold their wool, most of the cash went on rent—but selling wool made rent-paying easier, and left more to spend on other things. The wool trade brought greater wealth to the Scottish countryside, and at least a small part of that wealth stayed in the peasants' hands.

Source B: From a modern history book

> Before 1300, Scotland's valuable wool trade made it one of the leading producers in Europe. A country which could finance cathedrals such as St Andrews or Glasgow or abbeys such as Dunfermline or Dryburgh and lay out elaborate town plans such as those of Crail or St Andrews, and begin major royal castles at Edinburgh and Stirling, was not poor.

Source C: From a modern history book

Things to Do

1. How did ordinary Scots benefit from the wool trade?

2. How did the kingdom of Scotland as a whole benefit from the trade?

3. (a) What did the writer of Source A give to the Melrose monks? Why do you think he did this?
   (b) Why could a monastic order like the Cistercians easily arrange to sell wool overseas?

Scotland in the Middle Ages 400 – 1450 AD

Unit 10

The Wars with England

10.1	Who was the Overlord of Scotland?	93
10.2	Why was Scotland a 'kingless realm'?	94
10.3	Who was Toom Tabard?	95
10.4	What was Edward's plan for Scotland?	96
10.5	Who was the Wallace?	97
10.6	Who was Robert the Bruce?	99
10.7	What kind of leader was Robert the Bruce?	100
10.8	How important was the Battle of Bannockburn?	101
10.9	What was the Declaration of Arbroath?	103
10.10	How did the Church help Scotland in the wars?	105
10.11	Why did the wars last so long?	106

10.1 Who was the Overlord of Scotland?

IN THE YEARS between 1296 and 1357, the Scots fought a series of bitter wars against England. One of the causes of these wars was an argument about who was the Overlord of Scotland. Did the King of Scots rule his kingdom in his own right, or was he a vassal of the English king? When the king of Scotland was strong, he ruled as if he had no Overlord. However, when Scotland was weak, its freedom from England was put at risk.

The Historian
Volume 1 — Issue No.6

Scotland v England

In Source A we examine the claims as to who ruled Scotland

The Scottish Claim

SCOTLAND is the oldest kingdom in Europe. Its history goes back to the early kingdom of Dalriata and beyond. The King of Scots can trace his family line back through over a hundred kings. This can be proved by the rows of kingly graves on the sacred isle of Iona. When a new king is inaugurated at Scone, the king-list of Alba is recited. This list shows that the first King of Scots was descended from Scota, daughter of the Egyptian Pharaoh. The kings of the Scots are chosen by God alone and have held their kingdom in battle. They pay homage to the English king only for those estates which they hold in England.

The English Claim

THE kings of Scotland are our vassals for the land they hold in both kingdoms. In 1072 Malcolm of Scotland swore allegiance to William, King of England, to avoid certain defeat in battle. The Scottish King William the Lion was captured in battle in 1174. He paid homage to us and paid a ransom before he was released. The old Gaelic royal family of Alba died out in 1097. Since the days of Queen Margaret, the Scottish royal family has had mostly English Norman blood in its veins. Our Scottish cousins are a minor line of the same royal family, not a separate dynasty. Our Archbishop of York is leader of the Scottish Church. This proves that Scotland is not a separate land. The kings of England have conquered Wales and Ireland. They also hold Scotland by homage.

Source B: The homage of Alexander III in 1278

I become your man for the lands which I hold from you in the kingdom of England. No one has a right to homage for my kingdom of Scotland, and I hold it only from God.

Things to Do

1. According to Source B, why did Alexander III of Scotland pay homage to the King of England? Why did this complicate the 'Overlord' argument?

2. (a) Read both claims in Source A and discuss them with a partner. Which parts of the claims can be proved? Which parts are just legend?
   (b) Who do you think had the stronger argument? Explain your answer.

Scotland in the Middle Ages 400 – 1450 AD

10.2 Why was Scotland a 'kingless realm'?

DURING MOST of the 1200s Scotland was ruled by two strong kings, Alexander II and Alexander III. They kept the kingdom safe and mostly at peace.

Then in the 1280s disaster struck the Scottish royal family. The heir to the throne, Prince Alexander, died of sickness in 1284. Two years later King Alexander III himself died in an accident at Kinghorn in Fife when he fell from his horse during a storm. The new monarch was his three-year-old grand-daughter, Princess Margaret of Norway. A council of Six Guardians was formed to help rule the kingdom while she was still a child. In 1290 the Maid of Norway sailed from Bergen to the British Isles, but she died in the Orkneys. There was now no clear successor to the kingship of the Scots.

There were several powerful nobles in Scotland who had a claim to be the next king. One was the Lord of Galloway, John Balliol, a landowner with estates in Scotland, France and England. Another was Robert Bruce, Lord of Annandale. These were men with private armies and castles across the kingdom. When they heard the rumour of Margaret's death, these nobles began to collect their troops. This meant that there was a great risk of a civil war. In October 1290 William Fraser, the Bishop of St Andrews, wrote to the King of England asking for his help to keep the peace in Scotland. He also asked him to help choose the rightful King of Scotland.

Edward of England was a powerful king who also had lands in France and Ireland. In 1284 he had conquered Wales. He wanted to bring the Scots under his control as well. In 1291 Edward marched to Berwick Castle on the Scottish border at the head of a large army. He agreed to select the next King of Scots. A special court was set up to listen to the thirteen nobles or Competitors who had a claim to the Scottish crown.

> TO the most excellent and most revered Lord Edward, by the grace of God King of England, from his devoted chaplain William, humble minister of the church of Saint Andrew in Scotland. There has sounded through the people a sorrowful rumour that our Lady Margaret of Norway be dead, on which account the kingdom of Scotland is disturbed and the community distracted. On hearing this rumour, Sir Robert de Brus came with a great following to Perth, but what he intends to do or how he intends to act, as yet we do not know. The Earls of Mar and Atholl are already collecting their army. There is fear of a general war and a great slaughter of men.
> I heard afterwards that our Lady Margaret recovered of her sickness, but she is still weak. Knights have been sent to Orkney for certain news. If it turn out that our Lady has departed this life (may it not be so), let your excellency come with troops towards the border, to help save the shedding of blood, and set over them for king him who of right ought to have the succession, so long as he will follow your counsel. If Sir John de Balliol comes to your presence, we advise you to treat with him so that your honour and advantage be preserved.
> May your excellency have long life and health, prosperity and happiness.
> Given at Leuchars on Saturday the morrow of Saint Faith the Virgin in the year of our Lord 1290.

Source A: Letter of 7 October, 1290

Things to Do

1. Who wrote this letter and to whom did he write it?
2. What rumour had the writer heard? Why do you think he was not sure if it was true? How was he trying to find out?
3. What was the writer afraid might happen in Scotland? What made him think this?
4. What did the writer ask the person who received the letter to do? Why did he think this would be helpful?
5. Who do you think the writer wanted to be the next King of Scots? Give a reason for your answer.

10.3 Who was Toom Tabard?

EDWARD WANTED the next King of Scots to accept him as Overlord of Scotland. Most of the thirteen Competitors paid homage to Edward. Control of the royal castles of Scotland was also given to Edward, so that he could hand them over to the new chosen king. It was clear that Scotland would be ruled by a puppet king who accepted Edward as his master.

In November 1292, John Balliol became the next Scottish king. He had to swear allegiance to Edward and for the next two years Edward interfered in Scottish affairs. There was growing anger amongst the Scottish nobles who wanted King John to stand up for the rights of Scotland. Then in 1294 Edward demanded that the Scots send him troops for his wars in France. Instead King John signed an alliance with the French the very next year. He also withdrew his homage from Edward.

Edward was furious and invaded Scotland in 1296. He sacked the rich town of Berwick, even killing thirty foreign merchants who were trading there. He destroyed King John's army at the battle of Dunbar and quickly captured the key royal fortresses. John surrendered to Edward and was taken to Montrose Castle where he was humiliated. His symbols of kingship were stripped from him, and he was taken prisoner to the Tower of London. King John was remembered by the Scots as Toom Tabard or Empty Jacket.

> KING John was brought from Aberdeen to the castle at Montrose. Upon the King of England arriving there, King John was stripped of his kingly ornaments, and holding a white wand in his hand, he surrendered up to Edward all rights which he had to the kingdom of Scotland.

Source A: From a Scottish chronicle

> The nickname Toom Tabard came from the ritual humiliation inflicted on King John at Montrose Castle in July 1296. John was stripped of his tabard or jacket, hood and girdle. This was a ceremony usually performed on a knight found guilty of treason rather than on a king.

Source B: From a modern history book

Things to Do

1. How did Edward make sure that he would control the next king of Scots?

2. Why do you think the Competitors agreed to pay homage to Edward? Why do you think Edward chose John Balliol as the next Scottish king?

3. What forced the Scots to resist Edward in 1294? Why do you think they were especially angered by this event?

4. What was the purpose of the ceremony held at Montrose Castle in 1296? What was it meant to show or prove? What did King John's nickname mean?

Scotland in the Middle Ages 400 – 1450 AD

10.4 What was Edward's plan for Scotland?

EDWARD WAS now Overlord of Scotland. He wanted to make sure that Scotland was no longer an independent kingdom. It would only be part of his empire of lands in England, Ireland, Wales and France.

He marched through Scotland in 1296 and forced all the leading men of Scotland to swear an oath of personal loyalty to him. Over 1,500 lords, bishops and burgesses had to put their seal to the parchment document on which the oath was written. This became known as the Ragman Roll.

He took the Stone of Destiny from Scone. This stone was used to inaugurate the kings of Scotland. Each new King of Scots had to stand on the stone and be acclaimed by the nobles and people of the realm. The Stone was placed under the English throne in Westminster Abbey in London. All the regalia or special symbols of the Scottish kings were taken and destroyed.

The Great Seal of the King of Scots, used to authenticate official documents, was broken up. All the records, papers and charters of the Scottish kings were taken to London. In letters to other kings and to the Pope, Edward referred to Scotland as a 'lordship' or a 'land'. It was no longer to be called a kingdom.

He stole the Black Rood of St Margaret from Holyrood Abbey. This was one of the holiest relics in Scotland, as it was believed to be made from wood taken from Christ's crucifix.

No new Scottish king was appointed to replace John. Scotland was to be ruled by a Governor, John de Warenne, the Earl of Surrey. English barons were set up as sheriffs over the Scots.

An English Exchequer was set up in Berwick to collect taxes from the Scots and send them to London. Berwick was put under English control.

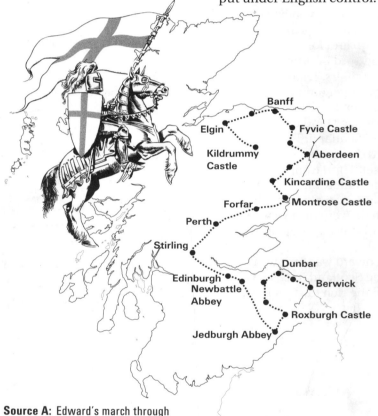

Source A: Edward's march through Scotland in 1296

Things to Do

1. Why do you think the Stone of Destiny was taken to London?
   Why do you think the Scottish royal records and charters were also taken?

2. Look at Source A. Suggest a reason why Edward marched as far north as Elgin.

3. Find out why the oath of loyalty to Edward became known as the Ragman Roll.

4. Look at the ways in which Edward planned to control Scotland. Which do you think was the most dangerous to Scotland's freedom?

5. How do you think the Scots would have reacted to Edward's actions? Explain your answer.

10.5 Who was the Wallace?

THE WALLYS or Wallace family were knights who owned land in Renfrewshire. William Wallace refused to accept Edward of England as his king and became an outlaw rather than swear loyalty to Edward. In May 1297 Wallace ambushed and killed the English Sheriff of Lanark. Some writers say that he did this in revenge, for his wife had been executed by English troops.

Wallace became the leader of a rebellion against the English invaders with hundreds of Scots flocking to his banner. In northern Scotland, Andrew of Moray pledged to fight alongside Wallace. Fighting from the mountains, they harried the English and began to win back land and castles from them. Encouraged by Wallace, other Scots began to fight for their freedom. In September 1297, Wallace led his men to a great victory at Stirling Bridge. They destroyed a much larger army, killing many English lords and knights, including the hated Hugh of Cressingham. Wallace was appointed Guardian of Scotland in March 1298.

In revenge, Edward led a huge army into Scotland against Wallace. At Falkirk the ranks of spearmen in the Scottish army were cut down by English arrows. After the battle, Edward toured Scotland again, forcing the Scottish lords and burghs to accept him as their king. Wallace resigned as Guardian but carried on fighting for Scottish freedom. He went abroad to Europe to try and raise money for the Scots' cause.

In 1305 Wallace was betrayed to the English and captured near Glasgow. He was taken to London and charged with treason. He argued that he was innocent of treason because Edward was not his king. Nevertheless, the English judges at his trial found him guilty. Wallace was executed at Smithfield in London. He was hung, drawn or disembowelled, and quartered. Pieces of his body were put on public display at Berwick, Perth and Stirling.

Source A: A statue of William Wallace in Aberdeen

ANDREW of Moray and William Wallace, leaders of the army of the kingdom of Scotland, to their beloved friends the mayors and men of Hamburg and Lubeck, be it proclaimed among your merchants that they may have safe access to all ports of the kingdom of Scotland with their merchandise because the kingdom of Scotland, thanks be to God, is recovered by war from the power of the English.

Source B: From a letter written by Wallace to the merchant towns of Germany

Scotland in the Middle Ages 400 – 1450 AD

IN the year 1305 William Wallace was craftily and treacherously taken by John of Menteith who handed him over to the King of England; and he was in London torn limb from limb and, as a reproach to the Scots, his limbs were hung on towers in sundry places throughout England and Scotland.

Source C: The death of Wallace

THAT same year of 1297 William Wallace lifted up his head and slew the English Sheriff of Lanark. From that time there flocked to him all who were weighed down beneath the unbearable domination of English despotism, and he became their leader. He was wondrously brave and bold, of goodly appearance, and boundless generosity. Wallace overthrew the English on all sides. Manfully he began the storming of the castles and fortified towns in which the English ruled, for he aimed at quickly freeing his country.

Source D: From a chronicle written in the 1380s

Things to Do

1. Why do you think Wallace rebelled against Edward? Do we know the real reason why he did this or can we only guess?

2. (a) How do we know that the writer of Source D thought highly of Wallace?
   (b) According to this source, why did people join Wallace in his fight?
   (c) Can you suggest a reason why this chronicle was written in the 1380s?

3. Read Source B. Why do you think Wallace wrote this letter? What was he trying to do? When do you think this letter was written?

4. Why do you think Wallace was so badly treated by the English? Do you think this cruelty was a good idea? Do you think Wallace was guilty of treason or not?

5. How has the sculptor of Source A tried to portray Wallace? When do you think this statue was made?

10.6 Who was Robert the Bruce?

ROBERT DE BRUS or Bruce was a powerful landowner in the south west of Scotland. He controlled important lands and castles. His family had long held the job of protecting Scotland's southern border in the west. However, Bruce also held lands in England. He had twice sworn loyalty to Edward. He had even fought against William Wallace at Falkirk in 1298. He may have been born in Essex and we think he grew up at the English court. He seemed to be a loyal vassal of King Edward.

Then in 1306 Bruce made himself King of Scots at Scone. He had a good claim to the Scottish throne. He was the grandson of one of the Competitors for the throne in 1292. Once John Balliol was no longer king, Bruce was next in line to be King of Scots. He was thirty two years old and already an experienced warrior and leader when he became king.

The Family Tree of Robert the Bruce

David I
1124–1153

Malcolm IV
1153–1165

William the Lion
1165–1214

Alexander II
1214–1249

Alexander III
1249–1286
=
1 Margaret & 2 Yolande

Margaret
=
Erik II of Norway

Margaret
Maid of Norway
d.1290

David, Earl of Huntingdon d.1219

Margaret
=
Lord of Galloway

Devorguilla
=
John Balliol

King John Balliol
1292–1296

Isabella
=
Lord of Annandale

Robert Bruce
d.1295

Robert Bruce
d.1304

Robert I
1306–1329
'The Bruce'

Edward

Nigel

Ada

Source A

Things to Do

1. Study Source A. Explain in your own words why Robert the Bruce was able to claim that he was the rightful King of Scots.

2. Look at Source A again. Say why you think Edward of England chose John Balliol as King in 1292.

3. Plan and design a wall poster about Robert the Bruce. Find out as much as you can about Bruce in your class or school library. The heading or title of your poster should be a question about Bruce eg. '*Did Bruce deserve the title Good King Robert?*' Make sure that you only include information which helps to answer your question.

Scotland in the Middle Ages 400 – 1450 AD

10.7 What kind of leader was Robert the Bruce?

WE DO not really know much about King Robert who lived more than six and a half centuries ago. We have very few records about him, although he is mentioned in some Scottish and English chronicles. A few documents bearing his seal still exist, but no pictures were made of him when he was alive.

Although we do not know much about him, a lot has been said and written about King Robert. For some he is the greatest Scot in history. Others have said that he was a selfish man, unsuitable to be a king and concerned only with his own rights. To make up your own mind about him, read the information below. This will tell you some of the facts of his life, and also what people alive at the time thought of Bruce.

FACTFILE Robert the Bruce

He murdered his closest rival for the Crown in 1306. He killed John Comyn, Lord of Badenoch, in front of the high altar in the Church of Greyfriars at Dumfries.

Most of the leading churchmen in Scotland backed Bruce's cause. The Bishops of Glasgow and Moray said that to fight for King Robert was the same as going on a Crusade to the Holy Land.

He carried on fighting even when his wife and sister were taken by the English as hostages.

He rewarded his most loyal friends like the Stewarts and the Douglases with large grants of land.

He never gave up the fight against Edward even when he lost battles at Methven and Dalry in 1306 and he had to go into hiding on Rathlin Island and on Arran.

He fought a vicious civil war against his Scottish enemies. In 1308 he ravaged the earldom of Buchan so thoroughly that it was a poor, desolate wasteland for years afterwards.

He waged war against a king who had earlier rewarded him. Bruce had twice sworn homage to Edward and accepted him as his overlord.

Bruce fought at a time when there was very little idea of 'the Scottish nation'. He was fighting for his own rights to the throne and lands of Scotland.

Bruce made himself King of Scots at a time when John Balliol was still alive, living in exile in France. Some said that this meant that Bruce had usurped or stolen the Scottish Crown from its rightful owner.

Bruce invented a new way of fighting which the English called 'secret warfare' at the time. Bruce avoided full-scale battles with the English. Instead he ambushed them, or attacked them at night, before vanishing with his men back into the hills.

Bruce was personally brave. The day before Bannockburn he fought and killed the English champion Sir Henry de Bohun in personal combat.

In less than six years, Bruce and his men skilfully ousted the English almost completely from Scotland, winning back land and castles that had been lost to Edward I.

Bruce planned a disastrous invasion of Ireland from 1315 to 1318 which led to the death of his brother.

Some of the leading Scottish barons tried to assassinate Bruce in 1320.

When he died in 1329 Scotland was a free, independent kingdom and at peace with England.

The Pope did not want to recognise Bruce as rightful King of Scotland because he had committed an act of sacrilege in Dumfries in 1306.

When he died his heart was taken in a special casket to the Holy Sepulchre in Jerusalem by his friend Sir James Douglas.

Long after his death he was called 'Good King Robert' by the Scots. They remembered him as a good, just ruler who helped to rebuild the kingdom after many long years of war.

Seal of Robert the Bruce

Scotland in the Middle Ages 400 – 1450 AD

10.8 How important was the Battle of Bannockburn?

THE BATTLE of Bannockburn is remembered as the greatest victory in Scottish history. The English Governor of Stirling Castle had agreed to hand the castle over to the Scots if no English army came to relieve him by Midsummer Day 1314. The new English king, Edward II, marched north with a huge army of 20,000 men which included around 3,000 mounted knights.

Bruce had always tried to avoid battles in open country, but now he was forced to meet Edward at Stirling. His army of 8,000 men was much smaller and had only 500 knights. However, the Scots prepared and fought well. Bruce chose a good place to fight. It was marshy land between the River Forth and the Bannock burn where the heavy English knights got bogged down. Hundreds of them were killed or captured for ransom. Edward fled south to Berwick, chased by the Scots cavalry. The English army was completely routed. However, historians have argued about the importance of the victory for Scotland and King Robert.

> The most important thing that happened in 1314 was not the battle near Stirling but the Parliament which Bruce held near there five months later. Bruce was now so strong that he could take away the lands of those who still opposed him. He also passed a law which made it illegal to hold lands in Scotland and England. The nobles had to choose which kingdom they would live in and which king they would obey.

> Bannockburn solved nothing. It didn't end the war with England. That dragged on for another fourteen years. The English refused to accept that Scotland was a free kingdom and that Bruce was its king. They invaded Scotland again in 1319 and 1322.

> For many Scots, the victory at Bannockburn proved that God was on the side of the Bruce. It was such a crushing victory that even Bruce's many Scottish enemies accepted that he was their true king. All the castles and fortresses in the land were turned over to him after 1314.

Things to Do

1. Why was a battle fought at Bannockburn in 1314? Why do you think Bruce did not want to fight it?

2. Read pages 101 and 102 carefully. Then make a list of the reasons why the Scots won the Battle of Bannockburn so convincingly.

3. Read the three different opinions about Bannockburn's importance on this page. Which one do you agree with and why?

4. Why do you think King Robert wanted to stop his nobles owning land in England as well as in Scotland?

Scotland in the Middle Ages 400 – 1450 AD

Timetable to Battle:

24 June 1314 was the deadline by which the English had to 'rescue' their men inside Stirling Castle or hand it over to the Scots.

10 June	Edward II of England calls his army together at Berwick.
16 June	English army marches across Border and into Scotland.
22 June	Bruce marches his army to their battle positions near Stirling. Most of the Scots are infantry spearmen, grouped in schiltrons or squares bristling with spearpoints.
23 June	Early morning. English cavalry reaches the Bannock burn, two miles south of Stirling Castle.
23 June	Midday. Bruce fights and kills the English knight Henry de Bohun in single combat.
23 June	Late afternoon. The Scots beat the English cavalry in a skirmish and force them to retreat.
23 June	Main English army arrives at the Bannock burn tired and thirsty. Edward decides to rest overnight and beat the Scots the next day.
24 June	Daybreak. Scottish army moves forward to attack.
24 June	Midmorning. English cavalry destroyed by schiltrons.
24 June	Late morning. Edward orders his archers forward but they are scattered by fast squads of Scottish light cavalry. Most of English army is crushed in on itself and panics. Edward flees and much of his army is slaughtered by the Scots.

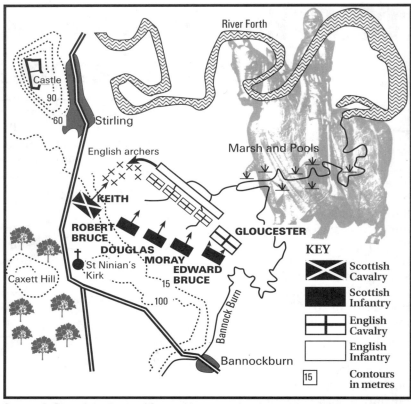

Source A: Plan of the Battle of Bannockburn showing the position of the armies at the beginning of the battle

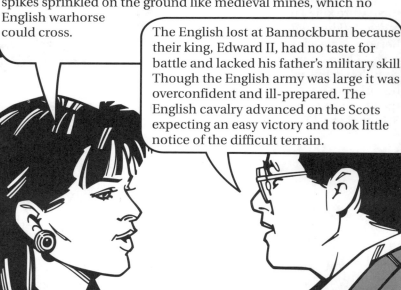

The Scots won at Bannockburn because of careful planning. We know that Bruce spent the day before the battle talking tactics with his chief commanders. The Scots dug pits to trap the English mounted knights. The Scottish infantry positions were well defended by long sharpened stakes and by caltrops, small iron spikes sprinkled on the ground like medieval mines, which no English warhorse could cross.

The English lost at Bannockburn because their king, Edward II, had no taste for battle and lacked his father's military skill. Though the English army was large it was overconfident and ill-prepared. The English cavalry advanced on the Scots expecting an easy victory and took little notice of the difficult terrain.

10.9 What was the Declaration of Arbroath?

IN 1322 KING Robert and Edward II agreed a truce. Six years later a proper peace treaty was signed at Edinburgh and Northampton. However, the Pope refused to recognise that Bruce was the rightful King of Scots. English envoys at the Papal Court made sure that Bruce was remembered as someone who had murdered an enemy in church.

In 1319 the Pope excommunicated Bruce which meant that he was cast out of the Church. The Pope also placed an interdict upon Scotland. This meant that priests in Scotland were not supposed to carry out duties such as baptism or burial services, a very serious matter in a medieval Christian kingdom.

The Scots wrote three letters to the Pope to persuade him that Bruce was the rightful King of Scots. The first letter was sent by Bruce himself and the Bishop of St Andrews wrote the second. The third letter was the most important though. This was the Letter or Declaration of the Barons sealed at Arbroath on 6 April 1320. It was written on behalf of all the barons, and the "whole community or commons of the kingdom". It was meant to show that Bruce was accepted by all the people of Scotland as their king.

The letter said that Scotland had always been a free kingdom. It put the blame for the wars on England and said that King Robert had been called by God to restore his people to liberty. The most famous part of the letter said, however, that if Robert ever accepted the English as overlords of Scotland, then he would be put aside as king. The Scots were fighting as a nation for their liberty, not just for one man. (see page 104.)

At first the letter had little effect on the Pope, but in 1324 Bruce was recognised as rightful king by the Church. Five years later the Pope allowed his son David to be annointed as the new King of Scots.

Things to Do

1. (a) Why was the Declaration of Arbroath written?
   (b) What were the Scots who wrote it trying to achieve?

2. (a) Read Source B on page 104.
   How does the Letter try to show that Scotland was an independent kingdom?
   (b) How does the Letter try to get the Pope to support the Scots rather than the English?
   (c) Why do you think the Letter emphasises English attacks on religion in Scotland?

3. Why do you think the Letter has been described as the most important document in Scottish history?

Source A: Arbroath Abbey today. The Declaration of Arbroath was signed at the Abbey in 1320.

Scotland in the Middle Ages 400 – 1450 AD

The Declaration of Arbroath

To our most Holy Father in Christ, the Lord John by Divine Providence Chief Bishop of the most holy Roman and Universal Church... from the lords, barons, freeholders and whole community, or commons of the Kingdom of Scotland.

...This kingdom has been governed by an uninterrupted succession of 113 kings, all of our own native and royal family, without the intervening of any stranger.

...Up till now our nation has lived in freedom and peace, under the protection of our kings, until King Edward, under the pretence of friendship and alliance, injured and oppressed us, at a time when we were without a king or a leader and when our people were unused to war and invasion.

...It is impossible to describe the injuries, blood and violence, the burning, slaughter and robbery committed upon our holy persons and religious houses, and many other barbarities which that king did to the people, regardless of sex, age or religion.

...At length it pleased God to restore us to liberty from these many calamities by our most serene prince, king and lord Robert, who while delivering his people and his own rightful inheritance from the enemy, did most cheerfully undergo all kinds of toil, fatigue, hardship and danger.

...To Lord Robert we are indebted, being the person who restored the safety of the people in defence of their liberty. However if this prince forget his principles and should ever agree that we or our kingdom be subjected to the king or people of England, we will immediately try to expel him, and make another king who will defend our liberties: For as long as one hundred of us remain alive, we will never submit to rule by the English. For it is not for glory, riches, or honour that we fight, but for freedom alone, which no good man will give up except with his life.

Source B: The Letter of the Barons, sealed at Arbroath in 1320

10.10 How did the Church help Scotland in the wars?

THE LEADING churchmen in Scotland supported King Robert throughout his long campaign. Bishop Wishart of Glasgow and Bishop Lamberton of St Andrews were close friends and supporters. They saw Robert Bruce as the best leader available in Scotland. Nevertheless they also had their own 'church' reasons for supporting him.

There was no Archbishop in Scotland. The immediate overlord of the Scottish Church was the English Archbishop of York. From time to time he tried to make sure that only Englishmen were appointed as Bishops in Scotland. Men like Wishart and Lamberton wanted the Scottish Church to be free from English control. In this way the Church and the people of Scotland had a common cause.

The Church's Role

- Church leaders went to Scone and made Bruce King of Scots in 1306.
- They stayed loyal to Bruce even when his cause was at its lowest ebb in 1307.
- Church leaders in Scotland ignored the Pope when he excommunicated Bruce.
- Churchmen helped Bruce to organise and run his first Parliament in 1309.
- The clergy openly supported Bruce at a General Council held at Dundee in 1310.
- Churchmen wrote many documents for Bruce, such as the Declaration of Arbroath in 1320. These were used as propaganda to win support for his cause.

Source A: Cambuskenneth Abbey near Stirling

Things to Do

1. Explain why most of Scotland's churchmen were on Bruce's side in the wars.
2. Why do you think Bruce held his Parliaments on church property like the abbey in Source A?
3. Why was it very important for Bruce to have the support of the Scottish Church?

Scotland in the Middle Ages 400 – 1450 AD

10.11 Why did the wars last so long?

THE WARS for control of Scotland began in 1296 and lasted until 1357. There were many reasons why these wars lasted for over sixty years.

✠ The English could invade Scotland but could never conquer it. The Scots could always retreat into the hills and wait for the right time to attack again.

✠ English armies seldom got beyond the river Forth. They could ravage the southern part of the kingdom but they were never able to subdue Scotland's heartland in the north and northeast.

✠ Once Berwick was lost, Aberdeen became the most important seaport in Scotland. It was very loyal to Bruce and too far north for the English to capture. Ships from Aberdeen were able to sail to Europe for weapons and supplies to keep Bruce's army well equipped.

✠ Scotland was only one problem which the English kings had to face. There were also rebellions and wars in France, Ireland, Wales and sometimes even in England itself.

✠ Even when the Scots were defeated in battle, they did not give up the struggle. They had a growing sense of Scottishness and believed they were fighting for a good cause.

✠ The English kept the war going because they would not accept that Scotland was an independent kingdom.

✠ The Scottish alliance with France worried the English who were always expecting to be attacked in the north by the raiding Scots armies.

✠ There were many Scots who were against Bruce. The Balliol and Comyn families, with support from England, kept the wars going in the 1330s and 1340s. It was 1357 before they accepted that they could not oust the House of Bruce from the Scottish throne.

It was difficult to maintain law and order in southern Scotland. The wars produced a great deal of lawlessness. There were too many men who had acquired a skill with weapons and a taste for action. These 'broken men' were a threat to settled communities, and a problem for the government, for much of the 14th century.

Source A: The effects of war on Scotland according to a modern historian

Farmland across southern Scotland was scorched. There was little point in spending time growing crops, only to see them burnt or carried off by raiders. Scottish farmers turned to cattle rearing. It was easier for peasants to hide cattle until the enemy had passed. But farming and trade were badly disrupted by the long decades of war.

Source B: Other effects of the war on Scotland

Date	Event
1284	Prince Alexander, heir to the throne, died after long illness
1286	Gude King Alexander died at Kinghorn in Fife during a storm
1286	Six Guardians appointed to rule Scotland
1290	The Maid of Norway died in the Orkneys
1290	Edward of England asked to choose next King of Scots
1292	King John Balliol chosen by Edward
1295	Alliance signed by King John with France against Edward
1296	King John defeated and stripped of his title
1296	The Stone of Destiny taken to London
1297	Wallace & Moray defeated the English at Stirling Bridge
1298	Wallace defeated at Falkirk
1305	Wallace betrayed and executed in London
1306	Bruce became King of Scots at Scone
1307	Bruce in exile on Rathlin Island off Northern Ireland
1307	Edward I, Hammer of the Scots, died
1308	Bruce destroyed the power of the Comyn in Buchan
1309	Bruce's first Parliament met at St Andrews
1313	Perth, Roxburgh Castle & Edinburgh Castle recaptured
1314	Bruce defeated Edward II at Bannockburn near Stirling
1320	Declaration of Arbroath sent to Pope John in Avignon
1324	Bruce acknowledged as rightful King of Scots by Pope
1328	Treaty of Edinburgh brought temporary peace with England
1329	Death of Good King Robert
1346	Scots beaten at the Battle of Neville's Cross in Durham
1357	Peace agreed between Scotland and England

Things to Do

1. Look at the reasons given to explain why the wars lasted so long. Choose the one which you think was most important and be ready to explain your choice. Say which of the reasons are linked and be able to explain the link.

2. Read Sources A and B. Make a list of the ways in which Scotland was affected by the wars.

Unit 11

The Kynrik at peace

11.1	Who were the Stewarts?	109
11.2	What was life like for medieval Scotswomen?	110
11.3	How were the Highlands different?	111
11.4	Who were the Lords of the Isles?	112
11.5	What was Scotland's Parliament like?	113
11.6	Did the Black Death strike Scotland?	114
11.7	What was the Auld Alliance?	116
11.8	What did others think of the Scots?	117

11.1 Who were the Stewarts?

THE STEWART dynasty or family was descended from knights who came from Brittany in France. Walter FitzAlan was friendly with David who became King of Scotland in 1124. FitzAlan followed David north to his new kingdom where he served in the royal household as High Steward. His family took the name of Stewart from this post. The Stewarts married into the Royal House of Bruce in 1327.

The first Stewart King was Robert II in 1371. His family stayed on the Scottish throne until 1603. In that year a Stewart, James VI, became monarch of Great Britain. The last Stewart was James VII who was overthrown in 1688 because he was a Roman Catholic. Members of the Stewart family tried to win back the throne in 1715 and 1745.

Historians have argued a lot about this dynasty. Most historians used to say that the Stewarts were, on the whole, weak kings and that they were an unlucky family. More recent historians have argued that the Stewarts were, in fact, skilful kings who did a good job of ruling the difficult kynrik or kingdom of Scotland.

Volume 1   *The* **Historian**   Issue No.7

The Stewart Dynasty

How successful were the Stewarts in ruling Scotland?

A traditional historian

ROBERT II and Robert III were weak kings who could not control their nobles. Law and order broke down. James I spent eighteen years as a prisoner in England. He was murdered in 1437 by rebel nobles. James II, who was only a boy of six when he became king, was killed when one of his own cannon exploded. James III was only eight when he became the next Stewart king. He was murdered by an assassin near Stirling after he lost the Battle of Sauchieburn. There were long periods when the king was just an infant or in exile. Powerful nobles used these opportunities to build up their own local power and to weaken the authority of the Crown.

A recent historian

MOST of the Stewart kings did a good job. There were far fewer rebellions against them than against the kings of England. Although there were very powerful noble families in Scotland like the Douglases, the Stewarts dealt with them skilfully. The Stewarts kept control of their kingdom at a time when other dynasties across Europe were being thrown off their thrones. Under the Stewarts, trade and the burghs prospered. The Stewarts were skilful propagandists who spread the idea of Scottishness amongst their people to make them more loyal. Even though some of the Stewarts were infant kings, the independence of Scotland was never in doubt while they were the ruling family.

Things to Do

1. Use your class or school library to find out more about the Stewart dynasty. Plan and design a timeline showing the main events in the history of the Stewarts between 1124 and 1460.

2. Choose one of the Stewart kings of Scotland from the list below. Find out about his reign as king and report back briefly to your class. Say if you think he was a successful king or not and be ready to explain your opinion.

   Robert II   Robert III   James I   James II

Scotland in the Middle Ages 400 – 1450 AD

11.2 What was life like for medieval Scotswomen?

THE EARLY written records do not tell us a great deal about the ordinary women of medieval Scotland. Most women, rich and poor alike, were simply expected to look after their homes and families. We know a little about some wealthy women who were the wives, sisters or daughters of kings and nobles. Queen Margaret is one example. Women were sometimes remembered when they acted in a manly way in times of war or trouble, like Black Agnes or Catherine Douglas who was known as Kate Barlass. One Scotswoman, Lady Devorguilla Balliol, was famous because she left money to build a college for Scots scholars at Oxford University in 1282.

After 1400, ordinary women appear more often in the records. There were women of the merchant class who had their own fortune. The wives of farmers could hold land. We have wedding contracts and bills which tell us something about marriage in medieval Scotland. However, poor women often appear only in court records when they were being punished for breaking the law.

> In 1337 the Countess of March and Dunbar was a dark skinned woman called Agnes. Her castle home at Dunbar was attacked by the English under Lord Salisbury while her husband was away. She led her garrison troops in its defence, bravely striding along the battlements each morning and taunting the English archers below the castle walls. She encouraged her men to hold out for five long months of siege until the invader retreated homewards. Salisbury lamented his failure: "Came I early, came I late, found I Black Agnes at the gate."

Source A: From a nineteenth century history book

> BESSIE TAILIFOUR, having insulted Thomas Hunter, merchant, by saying he had in his house a false measure which was found to be not true, she was sentenced to have her head placed in the branks and to stand at the mercat cross for an hour.

Source B: From the court records of the burgh of Canongate

> 34 ells of velvet
> 2 pieces of fustian
> 3 pieces of chequered cloth
> 50lbs of almonds
> 50lbs of rice
> 17lbs of pepper
> 1 roll of canvas.

Source C: Goods bought in the Low Countries for Mistress Janet Paterson in 1495

Things to Do

1. Why do you think we know a lot about Black Agnes, but not much about the daily lives of ordinary Scotswomen?
2. Read Source C. What sort of woman do you think Janet Paterson was? Explain your answer.
3. Read Source B. What happened to Bessie Tailifour? Why was this done to her?
4. Find out more about Devorguilla Balliol and Catherine Douglas.

11.3 How were the Highlands different?

AT THE TIME of the Norse invasions, large parts of northern and western Scotland were lost to the Scottish kings. These lands were owned by the kings of Norway, though real power was often held by local chieftains. The greatest of these was Somerled who attacked Renfrew in 1164 with an army of Highland, Norse and Irish warriors.

The Highlands were very distant and different from the towns of Lowland Scotland. Many ideas and changes that came north from England made little progress into these remote, mountainous lands. Gaelic was the main language here, not the Scottis or Ynglesh or French spoken in the towns. The Gaelic lords held court where sagas were still told by their bards and old Celtic traditions died very slowly. Although the Highland lords loved war, they also cherished music, poetry and learning. They encouraged the arts and science at their Court.

The Highland chiefs were a threat to the Kings of Scots. William the Lion battled to bring Highland districts like Ross under control. A skilful king like Alexander II made sure that native Gaelic princes were invited to his Court, as well as the feudal Norman barons who held the Lowlands.

The Western Isles became Scottish in 1266, but the King of Scots was still a distant lord. Throughout the Middle Ages, strong leaders like Angus Og and John of Islay rose up in the west to rule this kingdom of mountain, sealoch and isle.

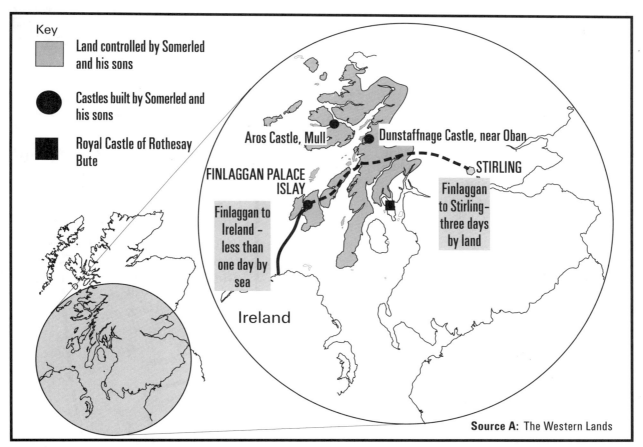

Source A: The Western Lands

Things to Do

1. Find two ways in which Highland life was different from life in the rest of Scotland.
2. Give two reasons which explain why the Highlands were different from the rest of Scotland.
3. Use your own knowledge, the text above and Source A to write a short essay called "Why were Lowland and Highland Scotland so different?"
   Plan your essay under the following headings: *the land, leaders, language* and *customs*.

Scotland in the Middle Ages 400 – 1450 AD

11.4 Who were the Lords of the Isles?

THE WARS with Scotland and England gave the Highland chieftains a chance to build up their own power. The MacDougall family supported John Balliol and did well when he was in power. Angus Og was on the Bruce side and was granted lordship over many Highland areas by a grateful King Robert.

By 1400 the MacDonalds were the most powerful princes in the west and were even called kings in the old Irish chronicles. Donald MacDonald marched into the north eastern Lowlands in 1411 to extend his power. He was only stopped at the bitter battle of Harlaw in Aberdeenshire.

John MacDonald became Lord of the Isles in 1449. He controlled almost all of Highland Scotland. He led a powerful army of gallowglasses, men who served as soldiers in return for land. They fought with the long Lochaber axe, the claymore and the bow. MacDonald was as powerful as the Scottish king in Edinburgh and wrote as an equal to princes across Europe.

In 1475 the Scots discovered a plot between the MacDonalds and the English King Edward IV to divide Lowland Scotland in two. By 1493 the Scottish king had taken control of the MacDonald lands. The Lordship of the Isles was abolished.

Source A: Gallowglass troops

Source B: From a Scottish chronicle

THE battle of Harlaw took place in the year 1411 because Donald of the Isles, with ten thousand islesmen and his men of Ross, made a warlike invasion ravaging all the land, intending to sack the town of Aberdeen and subject the whole country as far as the Tay to his power.

Things to Do

1. Give and explain three reasons why the Lords of the Isles were a threat to the Scottish kingdom.

2. Why did the Scottish kings finally take away the power of these Lords?

3. Plan an investigation into one of the following topics: Angus Og; the Lords of the Isles; the Battle of Harlaw; Gallowglasses. Make up a question as your title. Think about where and how you will get the information you need. Be ready to report back to your class.

11.5 What was Scotland's Parliament like?

SCOTLAND'S EARLIEST kings had a council of close friends and trusted warriors. This council advised the king and helped him to rule, making sure that Scotland's customs were upheld. After 1293 the word parliament was used. Parliament comes from the French word *parler* meaning to talk. Parliaments were often called together during the long wars with England. King Robert needed parliaments to show that he had the support of the whole community of Scotland.

Three important groups or Estates attended the parliaments: the nobles, the leading churchmen and the burgesses. The burgesses were elected merchants from Scotland's main towns. They first attended parliament in 1326 when Bruce wanted them to approve a heavy tax on the burghs.

The Scottish parliament usually met wherever the king happened to be. There were parliaments in Perth, Dunfermline and Stirling. After 1400 it usually met in Edinburgh, about once every year. Parliament passed laws which the king wanted to bring about. It raised money for special events such as royal marriages and wars. Subjects could also petition the king at parliament and make special requests for his help.

Source A: A later illustration of the Three Estates

Things to Do

1. What were the Three Estates? How was medieval Scotland's parliament different from modern parliaments?

2. Look at Source A. Where did the King sit? Where did the nobles and churchmen sit? Which group do you think is sitting furthest away from the king? Explain your answer.

Scotland in the Middle Ages 400 – 1450 AD

11.6 Did the Black Death strike Scotland?

IN THE YEARS 1347 to 1350 a terrible pestilence or sickness spread across Europe. It killed more than a third of the people. This great plague was later known as the Black Death. In the summer of 1349 it swept through England causing scenes of horror in every town and village.

The Scots were delighted when they first heard about the disease down south. They believed that God was punishing their hated enemies. The Scots gathered a large army at Selkirk, ready to attack England. That army was scattered by the plague. The soldiers fled home to all parts of the kingdom, spreading the infection.

> IN Scotland, the fyrst Pestilens Began, off sa gret wyolens
> That it was sayd, off lywend men
> The thyrd part it dystroyid then
>
> Before that tyme was nevyr sene
> A pestilens in oure land sa kene
> Bathe men and barnys and women
> It sparryed noucht for to kille them.

Source B: From a Scottish chronicle written after 1400

> GOD and Sen Mungo, Sen Ninian and Senyt Andrew scheld us this day and ilka day from Goddis grace and the foule deth that Ynglessh men dyene upon.

Source A: A Scots prayer from 1350

Source C: Burying the victims in 1350

Scotland in the Middle Ages 400 – 1450 AD

IN the year 1350 there was in the kingdom of Scotland, so great a pestilence and plague among men. By God's will, this evil led to a strange kind of death, insomuch that the flesh of the sick was puffed out and swollen, and they dragged out their earthly life for barely two days. Now this plague everywhere attacked the meaner sort and common people; seldom the nobles.

Source D: From a Scottish chronicle written by a plague survivor

THE Provost and council forbid any person from the parishes of Currie, Under Cramond, Swanston and other parts to come into Edinburgh on the pain of death, because these parishes are known to be infected with the pestilence.

Source E: From the 15th century records of Edinburgh burgh council

The main remedy for those who are attacked by the inflammation is to pay vows to St Sebastian.

Source F: From the Book of Pluscarden Abbey in Moray

Things to Do

1. Read the text and study Sources A to F, then say whether the statements below are true or false. Explain your choice by using the information in the sources.

   (a) Medieval Scots believed that you could protect yourself from the plague by praying to saints.
   (b) The plague struck Scotland at the same time as England.
   (c) The plague attacked different classes of people in the same way.
   (d) There were no symptoms of the disease on the bodies of Scottish victims.
   (e) Medieval Scots understood that you could limit the spread of plague by quarantine laws.
   (f) Only 1 in 10 medieval Scots died of the Black Death.

2. Source B is written in medieval Scots. Try and translate it into modern English. Reading it out loud will make it easier to understand.

3. Look at Source C. What is happening in this picture?
   What message about the Black Death is the artist trying to get across to the viewer?

Scotland in the Middle Ages 400 – 1450 AD

11.7 What was the Auld Alliance?

IN 1295 King John Balliol made an alliance with France against Edward of England. Robert Bruce strengthened the friendship between Scotland and France in 1326. He signed a treaty in which the French and Scottish kings promised to support each other in any war against the English. This promise was called the Auld Alliance.

The Scots were proud of the Auld Alliance. France was the richest and most important kingdom in Europe. The Alliance showed that the French treated Scotland as an equal and as an independent kingdom. The English were suspicious of the Alliance and felt that they were being surrounded by two enemies.

Thanks to the Alliance, Scotland got money and troops from the French. A thousand French knights were sent to help defend Scotland in 1385. Nevertheless, the promise to help France also brought trouble to the Scots. In 1346 they invaded England to help the French but their army was destroyed near Durham at the battle of Neville's Cross.

Volume 1

The Historian

Issue No.8

THE AULD ALLIANCE

What did the Alliance do for Scotland?

Two Views

THE Auld Alliance dragged Scotland into unnecessary wars with England. Scottish armies were destroyed at Neville's Cross in 1346 and at Flodden in 1513 while trying to help France. As a result, Scotland was set back for decades. The Borders and Lothians were ravaged by English armies. This was not worth the little aid that came from the French king. Scotland was just used by the French. It made more sense for Scotland to make peace with England. As long as the English were afraid of an attack from the north, they would try to end Scotland's independence which they finally managed in 1707.

THE Auld Alliance was very important to medieval Scotland. It mattered a great deal to the Scots that they were treated as being an independent kingdom. The English just treated Scotland as a territory and never accepted that Scotland was a free kingdom. The Alliance was proof that Scotland was different and separate from England. It also helped to build the trading and cultural links to the Continent which Scotland needed. Without the Alliance, Scotland ran the risk of being absorbed into England.

Things to Do

1. Imagine you were a noble adviser to the king of Scotland. Plan and write a short speech, in your own words, urging the king to either continue the Auld Alliance or to make a new peace treaty with England instead. Use your knowledge of Scotland in the Middle Ages to think of as many ways as you can to convince the king.

2. Find out what happened at Neville's Cross and how it affected Scotland.

11.8 What did others think of the Scots?

MANY FOREIGN visitors came to Scotland in the Middle Ages. Some were envoys or ambassadors in the service of European kings or the Pope. Some of these envoys wrote reports, which have survived, about their time in Scotland. One famous visitor was Aeneas Piccolomini. He was from Siena in Italy and later became Pope Pius II. When he visited Scotland in 1435 on behalf of the French, his mission was to encourage the king of Scotland to attack northern England.

He sailed from the port of Sluys in the Low Countries and arrived at Dunbar in East Lothian after a stormy sea crossing. His first action was to walk to Whitekirk, where there was a famous shrine to the Blessed Virgin, and give thanks for his safe arrival. He met King James I and described him as "hot-tempered and greedy for vengeance." He thought the Court of the Scottish king was very simple and no more luxurious than the house of a German merchant.

Aeneas described what he saw on his travels around Scotland. Thanks to him and other writers from Europe, we have a better idea of what life was like for the men and women who lived in the medieval 'kynrik of Scottis'.

> THE land is cold and largely without trees. The common people are poor and uneducated. They stuff themselves with meat and fish, and look on bread as a delicacy. The Scotsmen are small of stature but very brave. The Scotswomen are white-skinned and beautiful and very prone to love. To kiss a woman in Scotland means less there than to touch her hand in Italy. They have no wine except what they import from France. They export hides, wool, salt, fish and pearls to Flanders. Nothing on this earth gives the Scots more pleasure than to hear the English abused.

Source A: From the Commentary of Aeneas Piccolomini

Things to Do

1. What kinds of information does Aeneas give us about medieval Scotland? Do you think he liked Scotland or not? Explain your answer.

2. Why do historians value the account of European visitors more than descriptions of Scotland written by medieval English and Scots writers?

3. Investigate the life and reign of James I. Find out why James was looking for vengeance against the English.

4. Imagine you were an ambassador from Europe to the Court of the king of Scotland. Plan and write a report describing everything you saw and experienced during your time there. You should mention why you were in Scotland, your meeting with the king, other important Scots you met, the burghs you visited and the things you saw as you travelled around the country. You should try to include as much information as you can from other units in this book.

TIMELINE: Scotland in the Middle Ages

400	Beginning of the early Middle Ages
400	Pictish kingdoms in north and east Scotland
400	First Christian missionaries working in Galloway
500	Migration of Scots from Ireland to western Scotland
563	Columba founds monastery at Iona
590	Kentigern working in Glasgow
600	British kingdom of Strathclyde
600	Picts become Christian
650	Angles conquer south east Scotland
664	Celtic date for Easter replaced by Roman date
685	Picts destroy Anglian army in Battle of Nechtansmere
710	Picts begin to follow Roman Catholic customs
726	Angus has his vision of the Saltire
795	First Viking raid on Iona
830	Wars between Picts and Scots
830	Viking settlement in northern Isles and mainland
843	Union of Pictish and Scottish kingdoms into Alba
850	Vikings control most of the Hebrides
900–1050	Age of the powerful Orkney Jarls
903–943	Reign of King Constantine II
962	Edinburgh and Lothians absorbed into Scotland
1018	Strathclyde absorbed into Scotland
1018	Border decided at Battle of Carham
1057	Malcolm Canmore becomes king
1070	Queen Margaret arrives in Scotland
1071–1072	Normans invade southern Scotland
1124–1153	Reign of King David I
1120	Augustinians arrive at St Andrews
1192	Scotland recognised as 'daughter of the Church'
1256	School of Grammar and Logic founded at Aberdeen
1263	Norwegians beaten at Largs
1266	Hebrides sold to kingdom of Scots
1279	First 'Bishop of the Scots' at St Andrews
1286	King Alexander III died at Kinghorn
1292	King John Balliol chosen by Edward of England
1295	Auld Alliance with France signed
1296	Wars to preserve Scottish independence begin
1297	Wallace defeats English at Stirling Bridge
1305	Wallace betrayed and executed by English
1306	Robert Bruce makes himself King of Scots
1314	Scots destroy English at Battle of Bannockburn
1320	Declaration of Arbroath states Scots' freedom
1350	Scotland struck by Black Death
1371	First Stewart king, Robert II, comes to the throne
1411	Highlanders march on Lowlands towards Harlaw
1412	First college established at St Andrews
1468–1469	Orkney & Shetland become part of Scotland

Index

A
Abbeys 18, 46, **64–5**, 84, 91, 103,105
Aberdeen 68, 70, 73, 75, 78–79, 106
Alba 8, **32–40**, 46–7
Angles 8, 12, 35, 35–8
Auld Alliance **109**

B
Bannockburn 30, 55, **101–102**
Balliol, John 95, **98**–100, 106
battles12, 37, 51, 95, 97, 100–102, 112
Berwick 53, **55–6**, 73, 76, 79, 81, 91, 94–97
Black Death **114–115**
Border 37
brecbannoch 19, 30
Brough of Birsay 21–2,
Bruce, Robert 94, **99–107**
burgesses **75–80**, 113
burghs 46, 48, 62–3, 66–68, **72–81**, 113

C
Caithness 13, 16, 24
castles 37, 42–5, 45,47, **50–58**, 79
Celts 9, 11, 38
Celtic Church **26–31**, 48
Christian church **26–31**, 39, 48, **59–70**, 91, 96, 100, **103–105**
Columba 19, 27, **29–31**
craftsmen 76–77

D
Dalriata **8**, 13, 29–30, 35, 93
David I **47–48**, 53, 64–65
Declaration of Arbroath **103**
Dunadd 7, 35
Dunfermline 38, 64, 91, 113
Dunkeld 13, 24, 25

E
Edinburgh 35, 38–9, 47, 50–53, 61, 79, 103, 113–114
Edward I 94–100, 104, 55–56
Edward II 101–103
England 26, 37–9, 43–48, 50–51, 55–57, 62, 64, 69, 81, 93–106, 114, 116
Europe 16–7, 26–7, 39, 42–43, 46–47, 60–66, **69**, 79, **81**, 91, 97, 103, 106, 114, 116–117

F
fairs 48, **78**
farming 40, 64, **83–91**
feudalism **46**, 95
food 8, 76, 83, **87, 89,** 117
forinsec **51**
France 26, 42, 45–6, 50, 64, 66, 69, 106, **116**
friars **66**, 79, 78

G
Galloway 26, 45, 50
Gaelic 33, 38, 40, 45–46, 48, 111
Glasgow 72, 78
guilds **76**

H
Hebrides 16, 20, 23, 45, 90, 111
Highlands 29, 84, **111**, 112
houses 75, 79, **90**

I
Iona 13, 19, 23, 29–31, 35
Ireland 17, 23, 26–7, 35

J
Jarlshof **22**

L
Lords of the Isles **111–112**

M
MacAlpin 8, 13–4, 33–35, 37
Macbeth **36**
Malcolm Canmore **38**
Margaret **39**
monasteries 18–19, 26, 28–30, 48, 64–66, 91

N
Nechtansmere **12**
neyfs **88**
Normans **42–8,** 49
Orkney 10, 13, 16–7, 21–4, 94

P
parish church **61–62**
Parliament **113**
Perth 12, 35, 79, 91, 113
Piccolomini, Aeneas 89, **117**
Picts **8–14**, 18–9, 26, 29–30

S
St Andrew **31**
St Andrews 31, 33, 35, 38, 60, 69, 103
saints 8, 19, 26, **29–31, 39**, 62
schools 60–61, **68–69**
sheriffs 43, **53–4**
Shetland 13, 16, 22, 24
Stewarts **109**
Stirling 50–51, 53, 55, 57, 79, 97, 101–102, 105
Stone of Destiny 35, 96
Sutherland 13, 24

T
Toom Tabard **95**
Tower house **57–58**
trade17, 19, 48, 64, **72–81**

V
Vikings 10, 13–4, **15–24**, 31, 33, 42
Wallace, William **97–8**
wapinschaw **54**
war 8, 12–14, 24, 33–35, 37, 42–45, **50–59, 95–107**, 116
women 39, 76, **110**
wool 79, 81, **91**

Y
York 12, 33, 62, 93, 105

Scotland in the Middle Ages 400 – 1450 AD